Home Run

A PRO'S GUIDE

TO SELLING YOUR BUSINESS

Home Run

A PRO'S GUIDE
TO SELLING YOUR BUSINESS

7

PRINCIPLES
TO MAKE YOUR COMPANY
IRRESISTIBLE

JIM CUMBEE JD, MBA

Advantage®

Published by Advantage, Charleston, South Carolina.
Member of Advantage Media Group.

ADVANTAGE is a registered trademark, and the Advantage colophon is a trademark of Advantage Media Group, Inc.

Printed in the United States of America.

10 9 8 7 6 5 4 3 2 1

ISBN: 978-1-59932-923-9
LCCN: 2018935506

Cover and layout design by Carly Blake.

This publication is designed to provide accurate and authoritative information in regard to the subject matter covered. It is sold with the understanding that the publisher is not engaged in rendering legal, accounting, or other professional services. If legal advice or other expert assistance is required, the services of a competent professional person should be sought.

Advantage Media Group is proud to be a part of the Tree Neutral® program. Tree Neutral offsets the number of trees consumed in the production and printing of this book by taking proactive steps such as planting trees in direct proportion to the number of trees used to print books. To learn more about Tree Neutral, please visit **www.treeneutral.com.**

Advantage Media Group is a publisher of business, self-improvement, and professional development books. We help entrepreneurs, business leaders, and professionals share their Stories, Passion, and Knowledge to help others Learn & Grow. Do you have a manuscript or book idea that you would like us to consider for publishing? Please visit advantagefamily.com or call **1.866.775.1696.**

I hope you read this book with a pen or pencil in hand and make notes as you go. The stories throughout are real, though the names and situations have been changed to protect the identities of the individuals and their businesses. But the stories happened as I relay them, and the principles you learn from them will come in handy when you are ready to sell your business, whether that be in a year, three years, or even later.

I dedicate this book to the memory of my late dad, Ed Cumbee. By example, he taught me so much about how to be a father, friend, and respected businessman.

CONTENTS

SECTION I

What You Need to Know
Before You Try to Sell

When you go on a business trip, you typically don't pack weeks, or even days, in advance.

If you are like me, before you head to the airport you pull out your luggage, put in the right clothes, get your briefcase ready, and head out the door in time to get through airport security. No significant advance preparation is necessary.

Make a note: that is not a template for how to sell a business. Selling a business is a sequence of events that unfold over a period of time. You probably know that already, but what you likely don't appreciate is you may not totally control the sequence of those events. So, you need to understand the circumstances that might precipitate a sale so that you can get ahead of the process. You also need to know how your business will be valued. And, finally, you need to know the kinds of buyers in the market and how they will look at your business.

Take it from a pro: if you understand these things *before* you are ready to sell, you will dramatically increase your chances of hitting a home run when it's your turn at the plate.

1

PREPARATION: DO IT NOW BUT DO IT THE RIGHT WAY

My dad might not have been happy that I decided to be a business broker. He was once conned by a business broker, so he didn't have a high opinion of them.

Early in his career, Dad was a successful sales executive with R. J. Reynolds Tobacco Company. In his mid-forties he wanted to become an entrepreneur, so he bought a small retail business in our hometown of Poplar Bluff, Missouri. Dad worked hard and built a solid business that provided a nice lifestyle for our family.

By his late sixties he was ready to retire. I had gone off to pursue a career in law, eventually going to Harvard Business School to get a MBA, and finally settling in Florida to develop real estate. I wasn't around to help Dad through his transition, but he later told me his sad story.

One day, Dad got a call from a guy who said he could sell his business. Having a retail business in a small town, Dad didn't have many transition options, so he decided to meet with the guy. What makes the story most remarkable for me is that Dad made few mistakes in his business career. He was a very cautious, intuitive guy; he had not built a successful business being gullible. This business broker must have spun a good yarn, because he got Dad to pay a retainer on the spot, at which point the broker said, "I'll be in touch soon."

Well, you probably know how the story ended. Dad never heard from the guy again. Never. Suffice it to say, after that, Dad did not have a positive impression of business brokers. If he were still living, I know Dad would be curious why I decided to become a business broker after my successful corporate career and a profitable stint as an entrepreneur. I can assure you, while sitting in class at Harvard Business School, I didn't expect that one day I would be helping small business owners transition into retirement. However, the memory of what my dad went through never left me.

But then it happened to me, too!

I had my own frustrating experience with a business broker. In 1989 I decided to buy a business in Orlando, where I was living. I found what appeared to be a good opportunity being represented by a business broker. I did my research and due diligence on the opportunity. Not long before I was scheduled to close on the acquisition, I found a material misstatement in the financials, which seemed to surprise the business broker. I remember thinking at the time that a good business broker should have found this problem and brought it to my attention. But it also occurred to me the broker might have known about the material misstatement and chosen to not tell me. Bottom line: the business broker was either misinformed or unscrupulous. I didn't complete that acquisition, but it was a lesson in realizing there had to be a better way.

That experience soured me against dealing with a business broker ever again, especially coming after Dad's bad experience. At that point I set aside my entrepreneurial dreams, and moved on to a successful career with a division of the Walt Disney Company. I finally got around to fulfilling my entrepreneurial instincts when I resigned from Disney in 1995 to buy a radio business in Nashville. I made three additional acquisitions over the next six months. One of those businesses was in bankruptcy, which I acquired through the trustee-led auction process.

Boy, howdy! I sure learned that being an entrepreneur isn't as glamorous as I expected. But I had a great team around me and we had a lot of fun. In just four years I consolidated those separate acquisitions into one business that I sold for more than I had ever expected. At that point, I joined Salem Communications to handle its expansion into digital media, primarily through acquisitions. Through all of these experiences, I have observed (or been directly involved with) the transition of many small businesses. Amazingly, I realized Dad's bad experience and my own bad experience were not unique. The business brokerage industry is broken. There are only a few states that regulate business brokerage (if you can call them regulations). There are no standards of operation. Business valuations are a Wild West kind of experience. There are no peer groups that maintain quality control over business broker behavior or standards of practice.

The business brokerage industry is broken.

So, who is out there to protect business owners when they are ready to sell and transition into retirement? Well, no one. And that's why I decided to become a business broker in the last phase of my career. So, actually, I think Dad *would* have been proud that I decided to do this kind of work. If he were still alive, I know he would tell me to always tell the truth, never take advantage of people, and work hard. That's better advice than anything I learned at Harvard Business School, although the disciplines I learned there—such as rigorous financial analysis and thoughtful strategic planning—have proven exceedingly useful over my business career. I now bring all of my training and experience to help owners through the sale of their business, and transition into retirement or the next chapter of their career.

I have worked on business transitions in health care, manufacturing, media, retail, professional services, technology, entertainment, and education. While every business is different and every owner's situation is unique, they share commonalities that have led to the development of this book. I didn't discover these common principles in a classroom, but instead through the real work of buying and selling businesses. I call these the Seven Principles of Irresistibility. If and when a buyer sees a business for sale that has most or all of these seven principles, the buyer will pay a premium for the business. Every time. Guaranteed home run.

PREPARE FOR THE TIME YOU HAVE TO PULL IT ALL TOGETHER

Baseball was part of my growing up. Whether I was playing backyard ball with my pals from the O'Neal School or listening to Harry Caray call St. Louis Cardinal games on the radio, I always imagined that one day I'd be at the plate, taking a swing to win the World Series for my favorite team. My plan collided with reality somewhere in middle school, when I realized I did not have the talent to go as far as my dreams wanted to take me. But that sense of coming to the plate with all the pressure on the line to win it big has never really left me. When I decided to resign from Disney to pursue my entrepreneurial dreams by buying a radio company, I knew the time would come when I'd sell the company. Boy, oh boy, did I have dreams of hitting it out of the park, when all the sacrifice, hard work, and financial risk would pay off. Dadgum! I could actually *see* myself rounding the bases years before it happened.

But that plan collided with reality, too. My trip to the plate, with all the pressure on me, happened far earlier than I had expected.

A change in Federal Communications Commission regulations regarding radio ownership made my radio station group more valuable (the laws of supply and demand kicked in, but that's a topic for another book). I did pretty well when I came to the plate; most people would consider my results a solid double, maybe even a triple. But a home run? Not really. Sure, I got a good price. I was happy and I enjoyed working the next nine years with the fine company that bought my business. But, in retrospect, I realize I sold my business for less than I could have had I done a few things differently. I realize now my mistakes were common. Now that I advise business owners for a living, I can help them not repeat the same mistakes I made.

You see, when it's *your* time at the plate, you will face the same pressures I did. While there are no screaming fans in a stadium during the sale of a business, you still face the pressure of knowing you have your family to consider, as well as your employees, customers, and suppliers. This might even be your one shot to fund your retirement. Said this way, when it's your time at the plate, you want to hit it out of the park. Let me rephrase that, you *have* to hit it out of the park!

When selling a business, the most common mistakes revolve around the lack of *the right kind* of preparation.

I KNOW A SUCCESSFUL Major League baseball player—I'll call him Tom to preserve the confidentiality of our conversation. Tom and I were talking about his dream to build a baseball training academy in his hometown. Tom did not intend for this to be a money-making business; he made plenty of money playing baseball. But Tom wanted to build this academy as a way to give back to his community, to help aspiring young athletes develop their baseball skills. Having been in the majors for more than ten years, Tom knew that success at the Major League level was all about preparation. But he wasn't just talking about hard work; he was talking about the *right* kind of preparation. During our conversation, Tom said something that really stuck with me: if there are two athletes who are equally talented and successful at the college level, the one who makes it to the Major Leagues might get there because the *quality* of his preparation, years earlier, laid a better foundation for long-term success. So success is not just the result of the *amount* of preparation (hard work), it's also tied to *how* you prepare.

That principle is the basis for this book. Most business owners dream of their time at bat, when they'll come to the plate to sell their business and collect a big check. They can visualize the happy faces all around, the slaps on the back, and the exhilaration of seeing that wire transfer hit the bank statement. But it happens like that only when a business owner has prepared the *right way*, well in advance of their time at bat.

TIMING IS EVERYTHING

You have an awesome responsibility as a business owner. Every decision you make, every action you take, every plan you execute (or fail to execute) can have a profound impact, not only on your life but also on the lives of your employees, suppliers, and customers.

As a business owner, you are part of a larger game, and you may not be able to control how the game is played, much less how it ends. I know, because I have seen it up close. In the past three decades, I have been involved in the sale of scores of businesses, big, small, and in between. Though most business owners assume they will control the timing of their exit from the business, in my experience, more often than not, outside events intervene that affect when and how they exit. Here are just a few of the unplanned exits I've seen recently:

- A 50 percent owner was forced to sell because he could not afford to buy out his partner, who was in turn forced to sell his 50 percent interest because of a sudden health crisis.

- An owner decided to sell because she didn't have the mental or emotional energy to run the business after the unexpected loss of her husband.

- An owner had to sell upon after learning he needed to become the full time caregiver for his wife.

I get these calls all the time, and I always hear the same two questions: "How quickly can I sell?" and "How much can I expect to get?" The answer to both is, "It depends." Are your financials records in good shape? Where is your business on the growth curve? What's the quality of your management team? How profitable are you? Are there technology or regulatory changes on the horizon? Is the business dependent on one or two customers?

What's the common theme? Preparation.

If you are taking notes, circle this statement: it is never too early to start getting ready for the exit from your business, because it's likely you will not fully control the timing of your exit. The way I see it, your decision to exit your business is like heading to the bottom of the ninth inning of your own personal World Series. All eyes are on you; this is your one shot at being the hero. You want to make sure you've done everything you can to maximize your chances to hit it out of the park. By "out of the park," I mean an exit on your terms that generates the maximum value for your business.

Having said that, I need to begin in a dark place, because there is a monster problem waiting to emerge in the life of every business owner, and it's the problem of premature exit. Here are the seven most common reasons business owners suffer from premature exit.

PREMATURE EXIT REASON ONE: DEATH (OR PENDING THREAT THEREOF)

If the business owner dies, the heirs may need to sell the business. But many business owners do not consider how the death of someone else, or the threat of a life cut short, can also prompt an owner to sell.

I once handled the sale of a business owned by an attorney who dabbled in side businesses. Richard found a golden opportunity with the passage of the Dodd-Frank Act of 2010, which required banks to get delinquent credit card debt off their books. He would purchase a file of these bad credit card debts for six to ten cents on the dollar, then would contact the debtors to negotiate a collection settlement.

Richard discovered that one-third of the debtors could not be found, and another third were deadbeats who would never pay. The remaining third were good people who had, for whatever reason, gotten in over their heads. Perhaps they'd lost a job or had major medical problems. They wanted to pay their debt and rebuild their credit rating. Richard would coordinate payment terms with them. The way the math worked, if that one-third paid 75 percent of their outstanding liabilities, Richard would generate a 100 percent return on his investment.

"Why are you selling such a great business?" I asked him the first day we met. After all, this was a thriving business, relatively easy to operate, and there was no shortage of bad credit card files to buy. Richard explained, "I have been in solo law practice for thirty years, and my wife has been at my side as my assistant every day for those thirty years."

Then he paused. "We have no children, and my wife has stomach cancer. We don't know how much time we have left together, so we are looking to simplify our life. That's why I want to sell."

What was once urgent or worth burning the candle at both ends can suddenly seem meaningless in the face of events that threaten to curtail precious and limited time with loved ones. Pouring your heart, soul, and long hours into a business may lose its appeal under such circumstances. Nobody wants to contemplate being in such a position, but having the option to sell quickly is a matter of proper preparation ahead of the crisis.

MARVIN'S STORY was the most dramatic I ever witnessed. Divorced twice with five children, Marvin was diagnosed with a cancer likely to take his life within six months. He called me and said, "I have to sell my business before I die or my family will go into a probate food fight. Can you drive up to my office today and talk about how to get this done?"

I walked into his office about five hours later and was shocked to see a man in his mid-fifties who looked perfectly healthy. Given his prognosis, I was expecting to see a sickly looking, frail man.

There wasn't much time for small talk; Marvin got right to the point. He explained that his growing company was making about $2 million per year in pretax income. He had a solid management team, and his company had staked out a leadership position in his industry. But Marvin knew if his kids started fighting for control of the business after he died, the whole thing could come unwound.

Marvin had done nothing to prepare, because, as he put it, "I thought I was healthy as a horse. I work twelve hours a day, and I have no hobbies because I'm having a great time leading this company. Why did I need to prepare?" The business was sold prior to his passing, but the terms of the deal would have been more favorable had we had a couple years to plan.

PREMATURE EXIT REASON TWO: DISTRESS

Business owners may have to sell before they expect to because they enter a season of distress. Any number of things can cause distress in a business: personality clashes, a collision of values, family conflicts, debts that can't be paid, or maybe just a legitimate difference of opinion about how the business should be run. If the owner and his employees cannot reach a productive and mutually satisfying consensus and get through the distress, the owner may realize their only alternative is to sell the business.

Distress comes at times and in ways you can't expect. Take the case of the man who owned a 1,200-acre nursery business in southeastern Tennessee. He sold shrubs to hundreds of Home Depot and Lowes stores around the United States. He was one of the largest providers of shrubbery to those mega-retailers. Business was good—really good—and he planned to pass it on to his son once he was ready to retire. But then the unexpected happened: three straight years of debilitating frosts essentially wiped out his business. He told me he was financially prepared to weather one, or maybe even two, tough seasons, but he had never expected three consecutive years of frost. The financial and emotional distress caused him to abandon his plan to keep the business in his family.

ANDY WAS TELLING ME about the exciting rise of the business he and his partner started in 1999. They both had a 50 percent share of a company that owned seven ophthalmology clinics in four southern cities. Although he was also a skilled physician, Andy handled the company's business affairs while his partner, Larry, focused on the quality of medical care. They had their business relationship figured out, and the business model worked quite well. They were making more money in a year than some doctors make in five. But Andy called me to help him and his partner figure out a business divorce that wouldn't leave behind a scorched earth.

"The drinking didn't bother me for the longest time," Andy said with a tinge of sadness. "Larry worked hard, so I figured he needed to blow off some steam at the end of the day. But it got so bad that a couple years ago his wife told him to start rehab or find a new family."

Andy went on to tell me Larry had recently completed two rehab stints—a total of twenty-four weeks—during which Andy made all the decisions. "I know it sounds self-serving, but while he was gone, the business just seemed easier and the staff seemed happier. All hell broke loose when Larry came back from the second rehab," Andy explained. While the rehab had helped Larry gain control of his drinking problem, he came back a different man. He was more difficult, more demanding, and more erratic. After about eighteen months of nonstop squabbles, Andy told Larry he wanted to buy him out, to which Larry replied, "No, I'll buy you out."

My task was to figure out an exit strategy for Andy and Larry that didn't leave a scorched earth. Because Larry didn't have the capital to make good on his glib offer to buy the business, Andy's only options were to buy out Larry or stay in the dysfunctional relationship and hope something would change before the business went into complete collapse. Andy put together a deal to buy Larry's interest, but even now he admits it was a distress-driven decision he never wanted to make.

PREMATURE EXIT REASON THREE: DIVORCE

Divorce is a leading cause of premature exit from a business. I have seen situations where spouses are business partners, and, if they can't agree on who keeps the business after divorce, they end up selling to a third party. I have seen situations in which one spouse has to sell their business to fund a divorce settlement. I have seen situations where after a divorce a business owner is emotionally and financially out of steam with no energy left to run the business.

I once helped a couple going through divorce unwind from their business. They met while in pharmacy school at the University of Mississippi, and they bought a small pharmacy in the wife's hometown right after graduation. They were a good business team, and it wasn't long before they were making good money. When they learned they could not have biological children, the wife went into depression and made some choices that drove a permanent wedge in their relationship. Their divorce was not hotly contested; they wanted the marriage to end, and they both wanted to stay in the pharmacy business, just not together.

The only alternative was for one spouse to buy out the other, but that wasn't a viable solution since neither had the financial wherewithal to fund an acquisition. They ended up selling the pharmacy to a big-box retailer. She now works the night shift for the local CVS pharmacy and he has moved to another town and works in the Wal-Mart pharmacy. Their dream of business ownership came to a premature exit due to divorce.

Funding a divorce settlement is a common reason business owners come to an unplanned premature exit. A few years ago, a sharp business owner called me to say he had been ordered by a court to sell his company to fund a divorce settlement. When he negotiated the settlement several years prior, he agreed to pay his ex-wife a sum of money every year for five years. He made those payments for the first two years with no problem. The third year of payments was 2009. That year was at the heart of a serious recession, and he didn't have the cash to make the settlement payment. His ex-wife asked the court to intervene, which was her perfect right, and the court ordered the business owner to sell the company to fund the settlement payment. Suffice it to say, selling a business under a court order during a recession is no way to realize full value.

PREMATURE EXIT REASON FOUR: DISABILITY

A business exit isn't always driven by an event as dramatic or final as death or divorce. The decision to exit a business may be the inevitable consequence of a health crisis, be it that of the owner's or an irreplaceable member of the business staff.

Take, for example, one of my clients, Henry.

There I was in the middle of a meeting with Henry, walking through his steaming hot warehouse, when he decided to show me evidence of his recent heart surgery. Imagine my shock as he pulled up his shirt to show me his scar. Henry explained, "As I was lying in that hospital bed, I decided my business had gotten the best of me, and it's time to sell. I called you the first day I was back in the office."

No pressure, I thought. *If I can't sell this business, does this poor guy end up back in the hospital?* Henry went on to tell me he needed to sell this business or figure out a way to slow down. Little did I know how hard that was going to be.

After he pulled his shirt back down he said, "I've been doing this for thirty-four years, and I still haven't figured out how to find or keep good help. I have to do it all myself. Maybe that's why I had this surgery."

We walked back into the air-conditioned office to continue our conversation. "I'd like to sell this business and move to east Tennessee and help my son in his farming business. I know my health isn't that good, but, however many days the good Lord gives me, I want to be with my son and his kids."

On the positive side, Henry's distribution business had about 350 customers, most of whom had been with him for several years or more. There was bona fide demand for what he offered.

On the other hand, Henry was recovering from major heart surgery. And while he was emotionally ready to sell his business, there were other barriers. Because he had trouble hiring people he trusted, Henry was integrally involved in every phase of daily operations. And to complicate matters even more, the business's financial records weren't maintained on a timely basis. He also hadn't automated his business processes to leverage economies of scale. Henry was now at the point where he didn't have the time, energy, or capital to implement these necessary improvements before taking the business to market.

This was an unfortunate example of premature exit due to disability. Henry wasn't going to be swinging for the fences. In fact, he was going to be lucky to not strike out. With so much to do to get the business in sellable condition, but not having the time and strength to do those things, I told Henry that selling the business was going to be a challenge.

PREMATURE EXIT REASON FIVE: DISAGREEMENT

In businesses that rely on close contact and long-term cooperation between partners, outside pressures and forces aren't always the cause of premature exits. Sometimes the partners and their priorities for the business simply diverge as the years go by. If those divergences reach critical mass, the situation can lead to one or both partners deciding it's time to move on, as was the case with my clients, Rob and Hank.

"After all we've been through together, I can't believe the SOB tried that," Rob told me when we met.

Rob was telling me about the recent blow-up of his eight-year business relationship with Hank. They started their dental products distribution business in the middle of the 2008 recession, after both had lost their jobs in banking. In those days, making payroll had been their only concern, and every week was a struggle to economically survive. Thinking about the future (much less a successful future) had never been on Rob and Hank's radar. They never thought to create a partnership dissolution plan, until they had to.

It seems Hank had sort of gone rogue, signing leases for warehouses in two new cities and even making a couple of new hires—all without Rob's input. Rob was not a happy camper. He wanted out, and his preferred method was to buy out Hank. Hank wanted out too, but was expecting a hefty valuation.

I told Rob he had three choices. First, he could do nothing and let Hank stew for a while. Maybe time would heal the wounds or make Hank more realistic about his valuation expectations. Admittedly, this stick-your-head-in-the-sand approach rarely turns out well. Rob's second choice was to pay Hank what he wanted and just be done with it. While overpaying for a business is not an idea I often propose, I told Rob he should consider the cost of the problem *not* getting resolved. Paying a premium to be done with a problem may be worth it, especially considering you cannot place a dollar value on peace of mind. Rob's other alternative was to retain a mediator to help the parties reach a compromise. But mediation works only if the parties in disagreement agree to share the cost of the mediator, and mutually commit to good-faith efforts to reach a solution.

Unfortunately, I don't have silver bullets to solve this kind of partner disagreement, which I see all too often. It's not unusual for previously strong business relationships to head south over disagreements—quickly. Without documentation to chart a process for working through disagreements, these situations can lead to premature and especially painful business dissolutions. Even worse, they can rapidly turn litigious, which never ever ever has a good ending, even for the party that "wins."

PREMATURE EXIT REASON SIX: DISENGAGEMENT

Entrepreneurship is exciting. Until it's not. My client Russell knows this well.

"Well, truthfully, it's gotten to be a pain in the backside, if you get my drift," Russell told me initially. This was a clear case of business owner disengagement. Although we had a 6:30 a.m. meeting at Starbucks, Russell didn't need coffee. He lived a caffeinated life, running at a fast pace. The success of his company was evidence of that.

He went on to describe how the loss of a key staff member had forced him to spend less time on the design and engineering process he loved, and now more time on accounting and sales management. The change in his daily activities was wearing on him.

"I can do that stuff okay," he said. "It's just not my strong suit." Russell knew his growing disinterest might be a sign it was time to sell his company. "To tell you the truth, Jim. I'm just kinda bored."

As any business grows, it gets more complicated, and there are more moving parts to manage. Russell went on to tell me that, as the business grew, he had to hire new employees and attend more conferences. He said, "I had planned to sell the business when I was closer to sixty-five, but I just can't keep doing this that long. I'm just not doing what I love anymore."

As a general rule, it is better to sell the business while the owner is 100 percent committed and things are moving full-steam ahead. I have too often seen the alternative, like Russell's situation, when the owner waits to sell until they are tired or bored, at which point the business has likely lost momentum. Buyers aren't stupid. They can sense when an owner is disinterested. I say it over and over: sell your business before you have to. If you are trying to sell your business while you are disengaged from it, the buyer will sense it, and it will not work in your favor during negotiation of price and terms.

> **Sell your business before you have to.**

PREMATURE EXIT REASON SEVEN: DESTINY

Finally, a premature exit might just be a result of destiny, such as an unexpected change in the industry, technology, government regulations, or maybe even your personal life.

I once helped a gentleman sell his profitable business because he was moving to be with his new wife. He had been widowed almost ten years when he met a woman on eHarmony.com. They dated off and on for a couple years before deciding to get married. The only wrinkle was, if they were going to make their relationship permanent, one of them would have to move, and she had a great job in another state. My client told me it made more sense for him to sell and move to where she was than vice-versa. "Believe me," he said, "if you saw her, you'd understand why I want to move." Now that's what I call *destiny*!

Although I loved my job and the people with whom I worked at Disney Development Company (a division of the Walt Disney Company), I had a longstanding internal drive to be an entrepreneur, to own my own business. Maybe I got that from my dad; he left a corporate job to buy a business when he was forty-five years old.

When I started looking for a business to buy, a friend helped me find a business in Nashville that needed energy, capital, and direction. It was a perfect fit for what I wanted to do. The business had many problems, but none were insurmountable. I resigned from Disney to buy this small company eight hundred miles from where I lived.

I planned to operate that business for at least twenty years, hoping one day one of my children would want to take it on. But, four years later, there was a change in government regulations that relaxed constraints on the consolidation of radio station ownership, which effectively drove up the value of *all* radio stations in the United States. Nothing I could have done would have allowed me to see that coming. But it made my company soar in value. Destiny caused my premature exit.

The bottom line is you never know what's around the corner, which is why it's *always* a good idea to be suited up, warming up in the batter's box, and ready to swing for the fences.

CHAPTER 3

THE ART AND SCIENCE OF VALUATION

It might surprise you to know that every Major League baseball game averages one home run. Across every team, every year, at every ballpark, no matter who's pitching, whether the game's at sea level, in heavy or light atmospheric pressure, or if the team is loaded with muscled power hitters or scrawny scrappers, there is one home run per game. That's an astonishing feat of the law of averages.

Swinging for the fences in America's favorite pastime tends to produce a predictable outcome. Similarly, while there are several methods for valuing a privately-owned business, short of extenuating circumstances, nearly all methods will land you in the same general ballpark.

Let me walk you through the process I use to help my clients understand how buyers look at and value a business. As a precursor, you need to understand that every situation is unique. Both quantitative and qualitative factors affect the valuation, and reaching a final price is always a bit of a dance between the seller and buyer. That's why I call valuation an art and a science; it's situational. The potential for a strategic fit within an overall portfolio of businesses may motivate a buyer to offer a higher valuation, while strong profit levels but high dependence on the owner's personal presence or business relationships can drive down a valuation. For every ying there is a yang.

While there will always be exceptions, here's the big idea (if you are taking notes, circle this statement): buyers buy future cash flow. Meaning, the essence of business valuation comes down to projecting future cash flows, then measuring the risk of those cash flow projections.

Buyers buy future cash flow.

Let's say a business has had annual revenue growth of 5 percent for the past three years, and cash flow has held steady at 12 percent of revenue in each of those years. Short of an extenuating circumstance, it's reasonable to project that future cash flow will closely mirror the historic cash flow patterns.

If you grasp the concept of future cash flow, you understand 85 percent of what you need to know to understand business valuation. To round out your understanding, you need to know two terms: EBITDA and multiple.

EBITDA

Earnings Before Interest Taxes Depreciation and Amortization (EBITDA) represents the pretax profitability of a business, irrespective of debt. It is considered in many cases a proxy for cash flow. For the purpose of this explanation, whenever I refer to EBITDA, you can think cash flow.

Here's a simple example of how to calculate EBITDA:

- A company generates $200 million in revenue, has $90 million in cost of goods sold, and $60 million in operating expenses. Included in the operating expenses are depreciation and amortization of $10 million, and interest of $10 million.

- Therefore, the company has a pretax net operating income of $50 million ($200 - $90 - $60 = $50).

- Assuming a 20 percent tax rate on that $50 million pretax operating profit, the company has an after-tax profit of $40 million.

- To determine the company's EBITDA, we start with the after-tax profit of $40 million and add back:

  - taxes of $10 million

  - depreciation and amortization of $10 million

  - interest of $10 million

The result is earnings before interest, taxes, depreciation, and amortization (EBITDA) of $70 million ($40 + $10 + $10 + $10 = $70).

It may seem a bit silly to take out expenses then add them back, but this methodology is intuitive once you've looked at a few financial statements. The result, called EBITDA, is the starting point to understand the business's valuation.

MULTIPLE

A **multiple** is the number by which you multiply another number to derive valuation. The word gets loosely tossed around in conversations about buying and selling of businesses. "I sold my business for a multiple of X." I use the word loosely for a reason, so be careful what you assume.

I was recently talking with a potential client who owns a fast-growing marketing company. He asked what multiple he could get if he sold his business, and I said in the range of five to six. He seemed quite pleased, but after a bit more conversation, I realized he was thinking a multiple of *revenue,* and I was thinking a multiple of *EBITDA.* I explained that valuations are more times than not a reflection of multiples of EBITDA, not revenue. Once we had that common framework of understanding, he was, not surprisingly, less interested in the idea of selling.

Another confusion about multiples is how they are determined. What makes one business worth a multiple of four and another business worth a multiple of ten? The answer is more commonsense than you might think: the buyer's confidence in the future cash flow performance of the business. The higher the multiple, the more confidence the buyer has in the future cash flow of the business.

VALUATION SHORTHAND EXPLAINED: EBITDA X MULTIPLE

Let's take a look at a hypothetical company to see how this all comes together. For the purposes of this example, we assume we are doing this valuation in early 2017, meaning the actual results are for 2013–2016, and projections are for 2017–2018.

	2013	2014	2015	2016	2017	2018
Revenue	4,750	6,055	5,925	7,000	7,700	8,500
Cost of Goods Sold	(2,425)	(3,225)	(3,145)	(3,700)	(4,000)	(4,400)
Gross Profit	2,325	2,830	2,780	3,300	3,700	4,100
Operating Expense	(1,625)	(1,689)	(1,745)	(1,975)	(2,215)	(2,400)
Net Operating Income	700	1,141	1,035	1,325	1,485	1,700
Add Backs						
Depreciation	750	525	425	500	500	500
Interest	30	45	48	50	50	50
EBITDA	1,480	1,711	1,508	1,875	2,035	2,250
Adjustments						
One-time Extraordinary Expense	0	35	0	12	0	0
Owner Discretionary Expenses	9	9	6	12	12	12
Management Replacement	(135)	(135)	(150)	(150)	(160)	(160)
Adjusted EBITDA	1,354	1,620	1,364	1,749	1,887	2,102

Over the past four years (2013–2016), the company's net operating income (NOI) has shown an upward trajectory; the slight blip in 2015 is not so troubling and I don't see any red flags in the future. So far, so good. I think this company should get a solid multiple. But, before I make that final decision, I have to determine Adjusted EBITDA. This process will be explained in more detail in chapter 8, but here's a quick summary. Starting with Net Operating Income, I add back interest and depreciation. Then I add back the expense to have someone run the business, because, in this example, the owner's salary was not included in the operating expenses; at the end of the year the owner paid himself what the business had made that year. So, to get a true picture of how much actual profit the business will generate, we have to subtract the cost to hire and compensate someone to run the business. For the purposes of this exercise, I estimated a general manager compensation and benefits package of $160,000 per year for the next two years. I also added back one-time extraordinary expenses and owner-discretionary expenses that are not likely to be needed once the business is sold.

The final step is to apply *weights* to past years' Adjusted EBITDA. We do this to accommodate swings in business performance. In some situations, the most recent year's Adjusted EBITDA is the most relevant and should carry 100 percent of the weight in the valuation analysis. In other situations, looking at the business' results over a few years provides a better sense of future earnings potential. Therefore, weights are typically negotiated between the buyer and seller based on qualitative characteristics of the business. Is it growing slowly or rapidly? Was a recent year affected by a circumstance not likely to be repeated in future years? Has the business gone through a period of adjustment? Each of these factors can affect the assigned weights.

A steady business that hasn't grown substantially over the past few years may apply weights that are relatively even, such as 20/20/30/30 for 2013 through 2016. This kind of static weighting assumes there will be no significant changes in the business over the next couple of years. But in our example company, weights of 10/15/20/55 for 2013 through 2016 were deemed reasonable by both buyer and seller, since the business's revenue trend has been strong and its most recent year is representative of its revenue potential.

In application, you see the Weighted Adjusted EBITDA is $1.613 million.

Weighted Adjusted EBITDA (in millions)

	2013	2014	2015	2016	2017	2018
Revenue	4,750	6,055	5,925	7,000	7,700	8,500
Adjusted EBITDA	1,354	1,620	1,364	1,749	1,887	2,102
Weight	10%	15%	20%	55%		
Total	135	243	273	962		
Weighted Adjusted EBITDA	1,613					

Weighted Adjusted EBITDA is the number to which we then apply the multiple to derive the initial valuation. A multiple of three would result in a valuation of $4.839 million (3 × 1.613); a multiple of four would indicate a valuation of $6.532 million (4 × 1.613), and so on. But what drives the multiple up or down? That's the next step.

You could pay a professional business appraiser $20,000 (or more!) for a report that drills into hundreds of contributing factors (and at some point, when you get serious about your big at-bat, it may be in your best interest to do just that). But here is a shorthand methodology to help you understand your valuation multiple. This method will help sellers and buyers set realistic expectations up front and help the parties make sure they are in the same general ballpark.

The Valuation Metrics chart on the next page makes the basic assumption the business is running an EBITDA margin between 10 and 15 percent. The diamonds indicate what valuation multiple (the vertical axis) to expect at a given revenue (the horizontal axis). This shorthand analysis assumes there are no dramatic mitigating factors.

To locate the applicable multiple, place an *X* on the trend line at annual revenues and then locate the multiple value on the left.

Valuation Metrics (assumes EDITDA margin 10-15 percent)

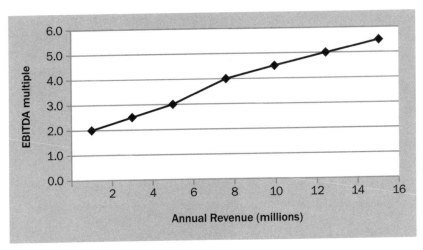

For example, with annual revenue of $7 million, the company's multiple would be approximately 3.75.

Now, let's go back to the Weighted Adjusted EBITDA of $1.613 million. If we multiply that by 3.75, we derive an expected valuation of $6.124 million. Another way to look at this is that the buyer could expect to earn back the purchase price in slightly less than four years. At higher multiples, the payback period would naturally be longer.

Putting this together is where common sense kicks in. Keep in mind, the multiple is not a valuation technique per se, but instead a shorthand way for a buyer to ask, "How much risk do I see in the company's future EBITDA?"

Remember what I said earlier? Buyers buy future cash flow (EBITDA). If buyers are confident in their EBITDA forecast, they might be willing to lower their return on investment expectation to 20 percent, which means they'd apply a multiple of five. If they think the business can grow much faster in the future and has untapped potential, they might be more aggressive and willing to pay an even higher multiple. Remember the principle: valuation today is a reflection of confidence in the future cash flow (a.k.a. EBITDA) of the business.

Now, there is another, more complicated way of understanding future cash flow valuation, and that's called net present value. This is determined by bringing future cash flow projections to "present value" by virtue of a discount rate. This is how big companies make capital allocation decisions, and at some point, you might need to understand this methodology. But for a basic understanding of business valuation, knowing how to calculate EBITDA and estimate your multiple is all you need to know.

What Might Drive a Higher Multiple? The Home-Run Valuation

For every rule of thumb there is an exception, and business valuations are full of mitigating factors that can increase or decrease the multiple. But the fundamental principle does not change: the value of a business today is a function of how a buyer views its future cash-flow potential. Getting a higher valuation (a higher multiple) usually involves one, or a combination of, these three factors.

- **Strategic buyer:** The buyer has a business imperative that is driving their interest in acquisition. This might be an interest in a key product line, specific customer, or special technology.

- **Accretive buyer:** When the acquisition alone creates value, the deal is said to be accretive. For example, when a company with a valuation multiple of nine buys a company based on a valuation multiple of five, the deal is said to be accretive. The difference of four is considered accretive value for the buyer, as the acquired company will be valued after the purchase at the same multiple as that of the company making the acquisition. So, a buyer with a valuation of nine can "overpay" for another company yet still create value, assuming they buy the company for a multiple less than nine.

- **Your company is irresistible:** Everything discussed so far about valuation has been quantitative in nature, but there are seven qualitative factors a buyer will use when assessing your company. If your company can check the boxes for all or most of these seven qualitative factors, it will be irresistible to a buyer and therefore sell for a higher multiple. These factors, which will be explored in upcoming chapters, are:

  1. Diverse customer base

  2. Sustainable revenue streams

  3. Reliable financial statements

  4. Demonstrable scalability

  5. Unique market position

  6. Owner independence

  7. Believable growth story

So What is the Value of the Company?

Given the company's revenue and profit margins, we preliminarily attributed a multiple of 3.5 to 4.0. But in our qualitative evaluation, let's assume we discovered the company also has a unique market position, a diverse customer base, owner independence, audited financial statements, and additional low-cost capacity (demonstrable potential scalability). These factors, along with the ability to potentially attract the right strategic buyer under the right circumstances, lead us to value the company at a multiple of six. Weighted Adjusted EBITDA ($1.613) × multiple (6) = final valuation ($9.678 million).

There will likely be working capital adjustments before closing, but in a nutshell, this is how the valuation process works. Armed with this basic understanding of valuation, the next subject for sellers to understand is the different types of buyers that are out there looking for businesses to buy.

WHO ARE THE BUYERS AND HOW DO YOU FIND THEM?

To look at him you would think he was past the point of retirement, but Harold was still going strong as one of Dallas's most successful business brokers. But beyond selling businesses, Harold was a business brokerage consultant. I spent a couple days with Harold early in my career, and I'll never forget something he said: "Buyers are the easy part of this business. The hard part is finding good businesses to sell." I was surprised to hear that, because I had always thought there'd be tons of businesses waiting to be sold and the hard part would be finding buyers. Well, many years later, I realized just how right Harold was. Finding good businesses to sell is the hard part; finding buyers is easy—with a caveat.

I hear all the time, "Who will buy my business?" and my answer is always the same: "It depends." There are three categories of business buyers: (1) individual, (2) strategic, and (3) financial. Each type of buyer has a different motivation and will value your company differently. Moreover, your post-sale role could be different with each. The starting point for understanding which buyer is right for your business is the size of your business and its rate of revenue and profit growth.

INDIVIDUAL BUYERS

If the business valuation is less than $1.5 million, the buyer will probably be an individual. An individual looking to buy a business contacts me at least once a week. That person might be a serial entrepreneur, or they might be tired of the corporate grind and ready to be their own boss, just as I was before I bought my radio company.

Transactions that involve individual buyers generally involve a commercial bank, and often that bank will coordinate with the Small Business Administration (SBA) for a guarantee on the loan. SBA guarantees are provided to help banks make loans they might not otherwise make. In theory, having an SBA guarantee is a good thing. Though an SBA loan comes with incremental cost, the borrower might not otherwise get a bank loan.

Moreover, not surprisingly, an SBA guarantee comes with strings. One is the requirement that the seller provide partial financing for the acquisition in the form of a seller note, and payments on that seller note have to be placed in full or partial *standby* (meaning no payments or only interest payments can be collected for two, three, or perhaps even four years). The SBA requires this to make sure the bank loan that is being guaranteed is paid first.

As an example, a business is being sold for $1 million. The buyer has equity of 25 percent, or $250,000. The bank provides an SBA-guaranteed loan of 60 percent of the deal value, or another $600,000. That means the deal is short $150,000, and that's the amount of seller financing—a personal note—the seller will be asked to accept. The SBA will require that no payments be made on that $150,000 seller note for two to four years, although they will allow interest to accrue during that period. Bottom line, when a business is sold to an individual and the deal involves an SBA-guaranteed bank loan, the payment terms might be more restrictive than the seller would like.

But remember the old saying, "He who has the gold makes the rules"? When using a bank to finance the purchase of a business, guess who sets the terms of the deal? You guessed correctly: the bank. Even if the buyer and seller agree on a certain price, the bank will not make a loan until an independent third-party valuation is submitted. More often than not, this third-party valuation will work against the interests of the seller. I've seldom seen a third-party valuation greater than the price agreed upon between the parties. Interpretation: when a seller does a deal with an individual buyer using bank financing, what gets negotiated in the letter of intent (LOI) is often *not* how the deal ends up being structured. Remember the golden rule: he with the gold makes the rules.

> **Remember the golden rule: he with the gold makes the rules.**

Let's see how this might work for that $1 million business. The SBA-guaranteed $600,000 bank loan will be amortized over ten years; at today's interest rate estimated at 6 percent, the loan payment would be $81,521 per year. As noted in chapter 3 on valuation, a small business is generally valued in the range of three to four times EBITDA. So assume this $1 million valuation came in at a 3.5 multiple, meaning the EBITDA was $286,000. So the individual buyer is investing $250,000 and committing to $750,000 in total debt to buy a business that is returning $286,000 per year. The buyer will have annual bank payments over ten years of $81,521 and, in year four, the buyer will start making annual payments on the seller note of $30,504 (assuming a six-year amortization, and a 6 percent rate of interest). Assuming the business doesn't grow, decline, or need excess capital, that business will return to the buyer an after-debt, pretax income of approximately $173,000.

Whether an individual buyer thinks this is a good deal depends on his or her income objective and confidence in the future of the business. Whether a seller thinks this is a good deal depends on his or her alternatives at the time the decision to sell is made.

STRATEGIC BUYERS

Strategic buyers do not start with an income number in mind. While they will be mindful of getting a reasonable return on their investment, strategic buyers have other reasons to make the acquisition. This is often referred to as synergy, a situation in which a combination of things end up creating something more valuable than each individual part. In deal parlance, you might hear synergy described as a situation where "one plus one equals more than two." In search of synergy, a strategic buyer will often pay more than the operating value of a business.

The strategic (synergistic) reasons a company might buy another include access to the selling company's customer base, proprietary product(s), intellectual property, or perhaps access to inherent economies of scale gained by adding the selling company's products to the buyer's operating infrastructure. I have also seen strategic deals completed just to get a competitor out of the market.

A perfect example of a strategic deal was the acquisition by my former employer, the Walt Disney Company, of Pixar in 2006 for $7.4 billion. At the time of the deal, Pixar's market value was about $6 billion. When the deal was announced, Disney said they paid the $1.4 billion premium because they wanted Pixar's innovative computer-generated animation technology, and their insanely talented staff of animators. But there were other strategic reasons Disney paid the $1.4 billion premium, though sometimes the strategic buyer won't come right out and admit the nature of their strategic interest.

Here's the reality of that deal: Disney didn't like having to compete with Pixar, and Disney was terrified another entertainment company might buy Pixar and create even more competitive pressure. Simply put, Disney had a number of strategic factors driving their interest in Pixar that justified paying the significant over-market premium.

I remember many stock market analysts saying Disney's over-payment by $1.4 billion was a mistake. In fact, the day after the deal was announced, the price of Disney's stock dropped. But Disney's strategic reasons for buying Pixar totally justified paying the 25 percent premium over Pixar's market value. Suffice it to say, time has proven that transaction to be strategically brilliant. It worked out beautifully for the shareholders and employees of both companies, not to mention those of us who love Disney/Pixar movies.

Now, here's an interesting nuance when considering an offer from a strategic buyer: if you don't do a deal with that strategic buyer when opportunity comes knocking, you might end up competing against that buyer.

As already mentioned, in late 1999 I sold my Nashville-based radio business to a strategic buyer, Salem Communications. At the time, Salem was acquiring radio stations throughout the United States, but it didn't yet have a presence in Nashville. Salem could have gone through the long and laborious process to get an FCC license to add a new radio station in Nashville, but it wanted to grow nationally and quickly, and buying stations like mine was in their strategic interest.

Salem wanted to be in the Nashville market, and I knew it was only a matter of time before they figured out a way to make that happen. Believe me, I didn't want to be competing against Salem's immense resources and know-how. So, while I was able to sell for a nice premium over my station's market value, I also won by saving myself from what could have become a competitive relationship. Said this way, the buyer was thinking strategically, and so was I, the seller!

Knowing it's possible a strategic buyer might pay more for your business than its inherent operating value, the next question is, how do you find a strategic buyer? Good news: the strategic buyer is often closer than you think. Perhaps it's a key supplier, a significant customer, another company in your industry that wants or needs something you have, or your competitor down the street. The point is, you probably already know other companies that could benefit from owning yours. The story of my friend Ralph best typifies this reality.

RALPH CALLED ME one day, almost in a panic. He described how he had just left a meeting with the president of a company that distributed his products. Ralph asked me to come to his office for a lunch meeting. When I got there, he closed the door, and said as he handed me a one-page document, "I thought he came to discuss next year's marketing plan. Instead, he hands me this offer."

I quickly scanned the document Ralph handed me. It was a proposal to acquire his company for a huge amount of cash at closing—no contingency, no earn-out, no seller note. Since I didn't understand Ralph's business, I couldn't figure out why this potential buyer was being so aggressive. Ralph told me that for the past five years, this company had been distributing a few of the products he created and manufactured. The distribution company's president told Ralph his products sold so well that they wanted to eventually sell all of Ralph's products, and have the first shot at selling products that Ralph and his team would develop in the future. This president and Ralph had been very close for a number of years, but selling his company to this man had never been on Ralph's radar. Ralph told me after the deal was done, "We were so close. I never saw him as a buyer." Ralph is now happily employed with that company leading new product development. The moral of the story: win-win strategic buyers are often closer than you think.

FINANCIAL BUYERS (PRIVATE EQUITY)

There are about three thousand and seven hundred private equity firms in the United States. According to *Bloomberg Businessweek*, these private equity firms have almost $1 trillion dollars of capital ready to be invested.1

The private equity industry is about forty years old, having grown out of the leveraged buyout boom of the mid-1980s. Remember the acronym, LBO? The hallmark LBO of that era was the KKR deal in 1988 to buy the stock of RJR Nabisco, converting it from public to private ownership. Soon thereafter, private equity began to take shape as an industry.

The driving motivation of a private equity (a.k.a. financial) buyer is—wait for it—financial: return on investment. More specifically, the core idea behind private equity is diversification of financial return. Private equity firms are managed by professionals with expertise in deal identification, structuring, and operations. High-net worth individuals and institutional investors (endowments, pension funds, insurance companies, etc.) are always looking for ways to generate

---

1   Sarah Jones, "With $1 Trillion Chasing Deals, Investors Park Cash in ETFs," Bloomberg Businessweek, Bloomberg L.P., August 9, 2017, https://www.bloomberg.com/news/articles/2017-08-09/with-1-trillion-waiting-for-deals-investors-make-do-with-etfs

higher returns while diversifying their investments. Historically, the only platform for diversified return on investment were the public equity markets. But in recent years, buying stakes in privately held businesses has proven to be an innovative way to generate returns greater than those available through the public equity markets. Simply said, investing in a privately owned business is a way to diversify one's investment portfolio *and* potentially generate returns higher than might be expected in the public equity markets.

But, investing in private businesses one at a time is inefficient, and this inefficiency has led to the proliferation of private equity funds. These funds are pools of capital from high net worth individuals and institutional investors who want to diversify their capital through an assemblage of privately held businesses.

Generally speaking, financial investors prefer to invest in privately held companies with an annual EBITDA of at least $1 million. Most private equity firms have specific parameters for the companies in which they are interested, such as a geographic focus or certain industries (health care, manufacturing, business services, etc.). But what all private equity firms have in common is their interest in finding privately held companies with four operating characteristics: a diverse customer base, a sustainable revenue base, an ability to generate incremental profitability on each new dollar of revenue, and a reasonably obvious growth plan.

This is not a three-out-of-four thing. Unless a company has all four operating characteristics, it is not likely to attract attention from private equity. On the other hand, when a company with these four characteristics goes to market, it is likely to find a number of private equity suitors. The owner of that company is for sure going to hit a home run upon exit.

While it's dangerous to generalize, it's reasonable to say most private equity investors are numbers driven. These are the kind of men and women who did well in math class. But, ironically, when selling a business to private equity, how a business owner communicates is every bit as important as the numbers. When you have a meeting with a private equity investor, remember to take both sides of your brain—the left side to explain your business model, and the right side to explain your vision for the future. Private equity investors are smart but they are also reasonable, and they want to be excited about your business's future.

It will also be helpful for you to understand the investment "thesis" that drives their interest in your company. One way to know if the private equity investors you are talking to are right for you and your business is to understand how they see your industry and your business model. If they have not done their homework to understand your market, competitors, and basic product offerings, they have not yet developed a thesis supporting their interest in your company. Simply said, without a thesis driving their interest, they are probably on a fishing expedition, so put them back in their boat and send them off to the next port.

Many business owners dream of the day a private equity firm walks in the door and makes a too-good-to-be-true offer. I can't say I've seen that happen often, but there is a compelling long-term advantage when selling to private equity—the opportunity to have a second bite of the apple. This happens when a business owner sells a portion of equity to a private equity firm, which then invests additional capital in the business with the intent to grow and sell it within four to six years.

I handled the sale of a technology company in 2014 in which the buyer acquired 80 percent of my client's company for mid-seven figures. The buyer had the capital and know-how to take my client's business and expand it into new territories. My client worked for the acquiring private equity firm for about eighteen months, but has since moved on to work for a private foundation at his alma mater. Meanwhile, he still owns the 20 percent of his company that he didn't sell originally. Once the private equity firm finishes its growth plan, it's likely (probable, in fact) that my client's remaining 20 percent will be worth more than the 80 percent he originally sold. Hence, he'll get a second bite of the apple.

But selling to an astute financial buyer is not all fun and profits. These buyers have very high expectations during due diligence, and once the deal is closed they are generally less sensitive to maintaining the culture of the acquired company, unless the seller can demonstrate how the culture itself is a value-added component. Said this way, things change once the financial players are running the show. I tell my clients if they sell to private equity, they have to be prepared to watch their company be run in a way they might not approve. Private equity buyers have their own systems, methodologies, and objectives, so if you can't emotionally release your company when you sell it, do not sell to private equity.

DON'T FORGET YOU ALSO HAVE TO PREPARE YOURSELF

I watched my son-in-law compete in the 2016 Olympic marathon trials in Los Angeles. Though he did not finish in the top three to make the United States Olympic team, I was proud to see him be part of this super-elite field of runners. After all, this was not just one race on one day for my son-in-law; this race was the culmination of fifteen years of brutal physical and mental training.

Selling a business is like running in the Olympics. The level of personal preparation before the big event is extraordinary. My son-in-law had invested thousands of hours in running, exercise, and good nutrition. He didn't just wake up a few months before the Olympic trials and decide he wanted to compete at the elite level. Had he done that, it wouldn't have worked out so well. Similarly, the business owner who wakes up one day and thinks, *I'll sell this year*, is likely to be disappointed.

Preparation is 99 percent of the difference between striking out and hitting a home run (yes, there's always a 1 percent chance you just get lucky). With a two-to three-year window before selling, there are seven things a business owner can be do to improve the chances of selling, and the amount for which the business will be sold.

1. KNOW THE MARKET VALUE OF YOUR BUSINESS

Most small businesses go to market overpriced for one of three reasons. First, an unethical or inexperienced business broker gives the owner an inflated expectation just to get the engagement. Second, I have also seen a business go on the market with an inflated valuation because the owner bases the asking price on what they need to fund their retirement, without any basis in market reality. The third reason I've seen a business go on the market with an inflated valuation is because of the owner's emotional attachment to the business; they simply believe it is worth more than it really is.

Spoiler alert: if the business goes to market overpriced, it is not going to sell. The market isn't stupid. You have to have an objective and knowledgeable understanding of your market value before you even begin the process. If you are being told by credible advisors the value of your business is not what you really want, you would be well served to not even put it on the market. Overvalued businesses don't sell, and the process will be waste of time and money.

2. REMEMBER WHY SOMEONE IS INTERESTED IN BUYING YOUR BUSINESS

In most cases, individual buyers are looking for a business with sufficient cash flow to meet their salary expectations. To be blunt, individual buyers are buying a job. Too often, a business owner will waste time with a potential buyer only to eventually realize what the buyer really needs cannot be met by the business. Before you spend too much time with potential buyers, ask specific questions about their objective and investment criteria. You might learn your business is not a fit for them or that they haven't given the slightest thought to those questions, meaning they likely aren't real buyers anyway.

3. BE OPEN TO CARRYING A SELLER NOTE

Many of the small businesses I see are not bankable in whole or in part, meaning a prospective buyer cannot get the amount of bank loan required to make an acquisition. There are many reasons for this, the most likely being the business does not have sufficient assets to secure the loan, or the business's cash flow is too unpredictable. In those situations, if the owner is not willing to carry a seller note for some portion of the purchase price, the owner is not likely to sell the business.

Here's how this might typically play out. The seller wants $2 million for their business. The buyer is an individual coming from a corporate job, and has a 401(k) with $600,000 and home equity of $400,000. The business has an asset value, including receivables, of $1.3 million. The bank agrees to lend $1.2 million, secured by the assets of the business and the buyer's home equity. The buyer is willing to invest $400,000 from his 401(k) account, so that leaves a gap of $400,000 if the seller is going to get the full asking price. The only way to close that gap is for the seller to take a note in the amount of $400,000. And remember, as we discussed earlier, if the SBA is involved, the bank will likely require that payments on the seller note be held in abeyance for two to three years. Unless this seller is financially able to do that, the deal will not get done.

I recently helped a client complete a transaction with almost those exact parameters. The seller had about $1.2 million in debt, so once that and his closing expenses were paid, he walked away from the closing table with only about $200,000 in cash. He will have to wait for that balance of $400,000 to be paid in the future.

4. BE PROACTIVE IN DUE DILIGENCE, EVEN BEFORE DUE DILIGENCE STARTS

Even if a business is correctly priced, bankable, and meets the needs of the buyer, the deal can fall apart if doubt enters during the due diligence process. Doubt is the cancer of due diligence, and once it has taken root, it's hard to get rid of it. Doubt comes in many forms: It might be something on a financial statement that isn't properly recorded. It might be concern about customer concentration. Or it might be something as benign as an errant comment from an employee or key customer. Once you hear doubt from your

> **Doubt is the cancer of due diligence, and once it has taken root, it's hard to get rid of it.**

potential buyer and/or the buyer's advisor in the course of due diligence, be quick to respond because, like cancer, doubt that lingers without attention can cause real problems. In fact, before you even put your company on the market, you should try to forecast areas of potential doubt and have strategies to address it. You have to recognize that problems do not get thrown under the rug during due diligence. They create a big ugly spot on the rug and, unless the problem is resolved, the deal will languish and likely die. That's called a strikeout.

5. GET PROFESSIONAL HELP

I love to watch professional golf. While it appears to be an individual sport, the world's most successful golfers work with a team of experts. Even the greats like Tiger Woods, Phil Mickelson, and Jordan Spieth travel with their coaches, physical therapists, and sometimes even nutritionists. As skilled and experienced as they are, these great golfers know that sustainable success is a team effort.

When selling your company, there is a cost to surround yourself with professional help. But you should think of that cost as an investment in getting the best deal for your company. I have seen time and time again how experienced professional support can help owners get more value for their company, not to mention help them create a more streamlined and efficient process.

Don't do what I did. When I sold my radio company in 1999, I did not use a third-party intermediary in the negotiation. I had a super-sharp lawyer when it came time to draft the legal documents, but otherwise it was me against the buyer. The CEO of the company buying my company had made, to that point, over fifty radio station acquisitions. This was the first time I had sold a radio company. So who had the muscle in that conversation? While I got a solid deal for my business, I probably left 20–25 percent on the table just by my failure to have an experienced third party by my side. It was my first rodeo, but not the buyer's; I should have been wise enough to get professional help.

6. KNOW YOUR WALK-AWAY NUMBER

I never take clients through the selling process until they tell me their *bottom-line* number, meaning if an offer comes in below that point, it will not be considered. I call this the walk-away number. I force the issue of defining a walk-away number before the sales process starts, because I have seen how the emotionally challenging process of selling a business can affect an owner's judgment. I never want a client to settle for something less than what he or she wants, just to get through the process or accommodate a hard-bargaining buyer. Negotiating experts call this the BATNA (best alternative to a negotiated agreement). Know your BATNA—your walk-away number—before you start.

The BATNA principle is different from the *what-is-my-business-worth?* question. Ninety-nine times out of a hundred, when I ask business owners what their walk-away number is they immediately reply, "You tell me. What is it worth?" That's when I have to explain that market value and walk-away are two different numbers.

KEVIN TOLD ME he wanted no less than $7 million for his medical services business, which was close to my estimated market valuation of $8.25 million (based on an EBITDA of $1.8 million). He told me if he couldn't get $7 million, he would be perfectly happy to continue running the business.

We had a meeting planned with a private equity buyer who was flying in to put an offer on the table. A few hours before the meeting, I called Kevin to discuss our strategy, knowing this buyer was serious and had the capital to get a deal done quickly. We knew the deal made strategic sense for the buyer, so we expected him to push hard on getting a handshake agreement over dinner. Kevin and I decided if the offer was below his $7 million walk-away number, we would not even negotiate. We were prepared to say, "No, thanks," and politely end the meeting. I have done this before and it always has the same effect. Serious buyers are not offended when a seller is willing to politely terminate a negotiation. They will either back off knowing the deal can't be done, or they will bounce back with a number closer to the asking price, and from *that* point the negotiation can begin.

But here's a caution about that strategy. Your BATNA walk-away has to be real. If you say you are going to walk away from an offer, you have to be prepared to really do it, to actually walk away. Otherwise, you expose a weakness in your negotiating style. As they say in Texas, "Don't be all hat, no cattle."

As for Kevin and this private equity buyer, Kevin was offered $7.5 million over dinner, and we negotiated the deal up to $8.2 million. Kevin didn't need to use our pre-determined BATNA strategy, but he was calmer and more confident during the dinner discussion. The buyer could sense Kevin was not going to be a rollover, and I think that contributed to his eventual home run deal.

7. KNOW WHAT YOU'LL DO AFTER THE SALE

It is commonly understood that more than 50 percent of business owners are unhappy about the sale of their businesses within a year of the deal being done. There are a number of reasons for this, but one I see too frequently is the business owner is bored and/or lonely after the sale. To mitigate this, before you sell, you need to have a clear view of your life after the sale. You may be surprised to learn that after you return from that long-planned trip to the beach (or to Europe, or the cruise, or whatever), you soon will be looking to replace the excitement of going to work every day. I know it might sound odd to refer to what you are doing today as "excitement," but even if you are frazzled and hate going to work every day, once you sell you will be looking for something to replace the activity. I don't see many former business owners who are permanently happy volunteering at church, taking the grandkids to school every day, or tending the garden with their significant other. While those activities are wonderful and worthwhile, they generally will not satisfy the emotional urge to be significant and create value. Think through this dilemma before you sell. Don't find yourself in that statistic of the bored and lonely.

Don't be like Henry.

Early in my career, I helped Henry, a brilliant forty-year-old technology guru, sell his company. He was making great money, and the business seemed to be running smoothly without a lot of effort from him. When I asked why he was selling, he simply said, "I'm bored."

We sold the company, and Henry got enough money to never have to work again. He and his wife had no children, and he told me they planned to focus their post-sale life on mentoring young technology entrepreneurs. Henry said he wanted to "give back," which seemed like a noble idea.

About six months later, I ran into Henry's wife. She was quite happy, having just finished a meeting with the local hospital board of directors planning their annual fundraiser. That kind of project was right up her alley, and her relaxed smile made it obvious she was in a happy place. I asked about Henry, and she got a bit of a sad look on her face.

"He's home, playing video games," she told me.

So I said, "He's developing a new video game?"

To which she replied, "No, I mean he's home playing video games. He says he's trying to figure out what's next."

I am confident Henry will land on his feet, but it is obvious his post-sale life plan needed some work.

Don't be that guy at home watching cable news, playing video games, or bouncing around at church looking for something to do. Before you start the selling process, have a plan for your post-sale life that allows you to engage your talents, experiences, and energy. Put yourself in the category of business owners who are happy one year after the sale.

SECTION II

Swing for the Fences: Seven Principles of a Home-Run-Ready Business

Now you know how businesses are valued, the types of buyers that are out there, and how to prepare yourself for your time at the plate. Let's now explore the seven factors that will make your business irresistible to potential buyers.

Think of it this way: buyers will evaluate your business with both sides of their brain. The left brain is the rational, quantitative side that will look at your business's financial history to evaluate its potential future cash flow and return on investment, as outlined in chapter 3. During this quantitative process, you might hear phrases like *risk adjustment, cost of capital,* and *capital structure.* Don't be intimidated; money people have their own language. But remember this, those money people also have a right side to their brain, which means they will also qualitatively evaluate your business. Too few business owners understand, much less focus on, these qualitative factors. But it's the qualitative factors that will determine whether your trip to the plate will produce a single, double, triple, or home run. If your business measures well on all seven qualitative factors, your business will be irresistible and you will enjoy a nice trip around the bases when you hit it out of the park.

CHAPTER 6

DIVERSE CUSTOMER BASE

When you're getting ready for your at-bat, diversifying your customer base is one of the first preparations you should consider. Taking steps to mitigate the risks of a concentrated customer base will not only increase the attractiveness of your business to potential buyers, but also strengthen your business in ways that are fundamental to its overall profitability and future growth prospects.

Here's how this plays out in reality. Imagine you are a prospective buyer evaluating two companies, each with $5 million in annual revenue and a 15 percent profit margin. You would think they'd be worth the same, right? Consider this: one company has five customers who spend $1 million each, and the other company has twenty customers who spend $250,000 each. Now I ask, though both companies have annual revenue of $5 million, which company presents less risk? Of course, the latter company with twenty customers is a less risky investment, and hence more valuable. It's logical and it's intuitive: the broader and more diverse your customer base, the more valuable your company.

Two brothers called me one day about selling their company that manufactures specialized equipment for commercial aircraft maintenance. In just five years they had grown the company to have annual revenue of $8 million by closely aligning with one of the world's largest airlines.

To say these brothers were intertwined with that airline would be an understatement. One brother had previously been employed by the airline in a management capacity, so he knew the operations inside and out. The brothers had wisely leveraged that insight, and with their ability to manufacture a dependable product for that customer, they were making great money.

When they were ready to retire, the brothers thought their relationship with that prominent airline would be a big advantage. What they didn't understand, however, was that because the airline represented 65 percent of their annual revenue, there was a huge risk in the deal. A rational buyer would be concerned that once the brothers were out of the picture, the company's strong relationship with that airline could end, and so, too, might that steady flow of revenue. Simply said, the brothers were overly dependent on one source of revenue. They had what we call a customer concentration problem.

The size and diversity of the customer base is one of the first qualitative factors a smart buyer will consider when weighing an acquisition. Businesses that are attractive to buyers ideally derive no more than 15 percent of revenue from any one customer. That way if one or two customers leave when the business is sold, the business will not face financial disaster. If your business suffers from having too many eggs in one basket, it can be one of the toughest issues to overcome when you want to exit. Therefore, start working on this as soon as you can; customer concentration takes time to resolve, and, if not addressed, will negatively affect valuation.

I once tried to help a woman sell her business (note the word *try*, meaning we were not successful). She had a very profitable business manufacturing fire retardant uniforms used by firefighters throughout North America. Her profit was about $1 million a year, and when we met she said she was ready to sell it for $3 million. Not knowing anything else, that seemed like a reasonable expectation.

But as the late Paul Harvey would say, "and now for the rest of the story." This highly profitable business had only one customer—literally one customer. She provided manufacturing services to a company that sold the uniforms to the end users. Her relationship was with that one customer, not with the hundreds of local fire departments that bought the fire retardant uniforms. My client had made a Faustian bargain: she was totally and completely dependent on that one customer for all her business, and in return she made a nice profit for manufacturing a high-quality, reliable product.

But when it came time to sell the business, imagine what prospective buyers asked: "How do we know the business's only customer will continue to use the plant after the sale? What if that one customer decides to renegotiate the contract?"

So, while her $3 million expectation made sense relative to her level of profitability, customer concentration made her business effectively unsellable to anyone other than, of course, that one customer. But that one customer didn't want to be in the uniform manufacturing business. They wanted to focus on sales and service, and they were happy to continue to outsource manufacturing. But since they were not willing to guarantee the contract for a new owner, my client was stuck; she literally could not sell the business. Ten years later, she is still going to work every day.

DIVERSIFYING A CONCENTRATED CUSTOMER BASE

To diversify your customer base, you may need to completely overhaul your marketing and sales efforts. This undoubtedly will take time and money. Take a hard look at what you've historically done to gain new customers, then explore additional means to reach new prospects in different industries, sectors, or geographic regions. If you've acquired new business primarily through referrals, now is the time to consider cold calling. If you haven't refreshed your website since 2013, now is the time to address it. Is your product mix old and stale? Is there something new you can add to your service offering? My point being, answers to these questions will help you broaden your customer base.

You can get a quick read on your customer base diversification by running a revenue-by-customer report for the past three to four years. More times than not, a prospective buyer will ask for this, so you should go ahead and have it prepared. It will give you a general sense of the state of your customer concentration. Then drill deeper: What industries and economic sectors do you serve? What is the geographic distribution of your customers? Is your business primarily local, regional, or national?

I HAVE A FRIEND who is the CEO of a company that owns several dozen stores that sell and install tires for cars and trucks. One day, he was describing challenges in his business that came from the coal production business. That didn't make sense to me, because his business had nothing to do with coal production. But he explained that many of his stores were located in eastern Kentucky and West Virginia, areas heavily dependent on the health of the coal production business. When the coal production business slows down, customers from those areas cannot afford new tires, and trucks used in coal mining are used less, which reduces the need to buy new tires. Although my friend's company had thousands of customers, they still had a customer concentration problem because their stores were concentrated in an area dependent on one vertical, coal production.

My friend's story is a powerful lesson about the need to peel back the onion when evaluating customer concentration. Diversification of customers is not only about the actual number of customers, the nature and source of your customer base matters. Imagine you own a McDonald's franchise on the Gulf Coast, and it is the first stop for guys coming off the oil rigs. You'd have a steady stream of hungry customers, and likely a very profitable business, right? But what would happen if oil prices declined and drilling slowed down so fewer men were being sent to and from the offshore rigs? You would have fewer customers because your customer base is concentrated in that one source: offshore oil production.

Some cities have a reputation for being difficult places to sell a business given the nature of their residents. Clarksville, Tennessee, is the home of Fort Campbell, one of the United States' largest Army installations, and the base of the historic 101st Airborne Division. The economic health of Clarksville will rise and fall based on the population of this Army base. During the years immediately after the September 11, 2001 terrorist attacks, Fort Campbell had a low population as the brave men and women stationed there were deployed to Afghanistan and Iraq. This had a negative effect on all the businesses in the Clarksville area, from car dealerships to restaurants and everything in between. So, if your business relied heavily on the Clarksville customer base, you were at risk of having a customer concentration problem.

Of course, it is common to start a business on the strength of one customer relationship. But, be aware, selling that business can be a challenge if you don't expand the base of customers. I recently consulted with a business owner who developed software for college prep testing in high schools. In the mid-1990s he worked for his state's department of education, and he could see how software was beginning to solve problems that had always been handled with paper, lots of paper. He left that state job to develop his idea to use software to solve this problem, and yes, his first customer was that state's department of education.

When he approached me about selling the company, that one state represented 60 percent of his total revenue. While that one customer relationship was quite stable (going on fifteen years), potential buyers were nervous about the company's revenue stability. We heard this warning from potential buyers often enough that my client decided to take his company off the market and put together a reinvigorated sales effort to add at least two more states to his customer portfolio. This strategy would work to his benefit in two ways: (1) the two additional states would solve not only his customer concentration problem, but (2) also increase his revenue. While this effort could likely take two to three years, it will ultimately be worth the investment of time and money.

The heart of irresistibility is predictability. The more predictable you can make the future of your business, the more value you can get when it's time for your trip to the plate. If your revenue is spread over a significant number of customers and those customers are stable, listen for the crack of the bat when you take a swing: that might just be your ball heading out of the park!

SUSTAINABLE REVENUE

"Every year, two-thirds of our subscribers renew, and many of them have been with us more than ten years." Dale was rightfully proud of the magazine he had owned for twenty-five years. He'd bought it out of bankruptcy, and over time figured out a formula his readers loved. Dale had built a money machine.

I was once retained to help a company interested in buying hobbyist magazines like Dale's. When I called Dale to gauge his interest in selling, he gave me his valuation expectation, which almost made me choke on my coffee. He wanted a multiple of ten! At first pass, his expectation was crazy. But when I studied his subscriber profile, I could see the publication's $2.5 million revenue stream was remarkably consistent. If my client bought the magazine and continued to provide the same quality of content Dale published, there was no reason to expect the subscriber base would decline.

Dale ultimately got close to what he was asking for the magazine because he was able to demonstrate that his revenue stream was sustainable. My client was comfortable stretching to meet Dale's expectation because we had evidence there was minimal risk in the acquisition. This is the universal principle to which we

Lower the perceived risk to the buyer, and buyer will pay more.

return over and over: lower the perceived risk to the buyer, and buyer will pay more.

Author John Warrillow coined the perfect question to help business owners understand the concept of sustainable revenue: is your customer automatic? (Check out John's terrific books, *Built to Sell*, and *The Automatic Customer*.)[2] Of course, nothing in life is automatic, other than taxes and death, but having a revenue stream that is reliable and predictable goes a long way toward making your company irresistible, just as Dale's magazine was to my client.

Let's recall why revenue sustainability is an important consideration. When potential buyers are looking at your business they are making a risk/reward tradeoff. The more risk they see in your business, the less reward they will give you for it. It's common sense. On the other hand, if the buyer can reliably predict future cash flow, the business is inherently less risky and hence more valuable.

Another risk/reward advantage to a sustainable revenue base is that customers do not have to be resold every time they make a purchase. Those customers may not be *automatic*, but they come back predisposed to buy, which lessens the cost of marketing and sales.

I once handled the sale of a prominent wine shop in an affluent area of Nashville. Of course, none of the store's customers were under contract, but the clientele was remarkably consistent because my client had access to a few premium wine brands not available elsewhere in Nashville. He had scores of regular customers who would come in frequently to see what was new.

Other ways to describe sustainable revenue would be revenue that is regular, predictable, or orderly. If you are older than fifty-five, you probably remember the TV show *Leave it to Beaver*. One of the show's

---

2   John Warrillow, *Built to Sell: Turn Your Business into One You Can Sell*, Toronto, Canada: Flip Jet Media, 2010; John Warrillow, *The Automatic Customer: Creating a Subscription Business in Any Industry*, London: Portfolio Penguin, 2016.

memorable characters was a guy called Lumpy. If you remember the show, you know "Lumpy" was a perfect nickname for him. "Lumpy" is the also perfect word to describe what you *don't* want for your revenue stream. A disaster recovery/restoration service is the perfect example of a lumpy business model. When there is a need for this service, such as after the hurricanes of 2017, there is a big spike in revenue. Problem is, you can't predict that need, so when there's not a need, there isn't much demand, hence the revenue goes down. That up and down with no predictability is the essence of a lumpy revenue model. Contrast that with a company that sells software on a subscription basis. This would be considered a smooth revenue model, meaning it is easier to predict and therefore more likely to be sustainable. Remember our principle: a decrease in future risk results in an increase in business value today.

Of course, there are many situations when a business has a blend of lumpy and smooth revenue. My former radio business is a good example. Selling advertising is a lumpy model. Advertiser demand tends to come and go based on the time of year and "daypart" you are selling. A daypart is a standard way of dividing up radio airtime and charging different rates for ads that run during those times. Drive time during the holidays is always easy to sell, whereas middays during the summer is a tougher sell. Overall, the advertising revenue of a radio station will be lumpy, i.e., have peaks and valleys.

But, in addition to owning radio stations, I owned a service that sold programming to scores of radio stations around the country. Those radio stations paid a flat fee every month for access to our programming. Once radio stations started using our programming, they weren't likely to stop making that payment because they needed access to our programming. That programming revenue came in every month with wonderful regularity. When I got ready to sell the business, the prospective buyer could see my revenue streams were nicely balanced, which, in part, helped me get a higher-than-market multiple on EBITDA.

When it comes to understanding sustainable revenue, nothing is better than an actual contract with a customer. However, you can demonstrate sustainability in a number of ways without having a contract. I once worked with a client who provided information technology services for midsized companies. The companies were under contract with my client, but the contract could be terminated with a sixty-day notice, so that did not necessarily prove revenue sustainability. To counteract any doubt on this issue, we developed a five-year revenue chart to demonstrate that 60 percent of my client's customers had been with him for more than five years, and the average length of stay for all customers was thirty-three months. In other words, we produced actionable evidence that potential buyers considered proof of revenue sustainability, assuming service and quality levels were maintained.

Of course, it's fair to recognize that what's perceived as sustainable by one party might not be for another. Said this way, sustainability is in the eye of the beholder. Chip owned a security monitoring business with 35 percent of its revenue coming from customers under a one-year contract, with the 65 percent balance coming from long-standing customers without contracts. I asked Chip why he didn't get the 65 percent under contract, and he said, "They know me, I know them, they know I provide good service, and I know they'll pay." I like that line of thinking, and it worked well for him given his com-mitment to customer service—until he got ready to sell. As we talked with several security monitoring companies that were in consolida-tion mode, we learned the industry-standard valuation methodology discounted the value of revenue not under contract. Even though we were able to demonstrate sustainability, we did not have contracts for 65 percent of the revenue, and that was a significant ding in our valuation. This example is not meant to say that you can't sell your business in the absence of contracts, but you have to appreciate that revenue sustainability means different things to different buyers.

I once handled the sale of a medical practice where the retiring doctor hadn't done an ounce of marketing for fifteen years (except for sponsoring his grandson's T-ball team). The buyer was concerned the patient base could evaporate after the doctor was gone. We pointed out that people who lived near this successful practice would continue to get ill and require medical service, so we didn't feel the need to prove demand. However, the buyer needed some kind of comfort that patients would continue coming to the practice after a new doctor was in place. So we did an anonymous study (closely following HIPAA privacy guidelines) to determine the most common conditions treated by my client. We realized that over 60 percent of his patients' medical needs were simple in-and-out visits. Our logic was that people would continue to get sick and come to a conveniently located doctor's office. Knowing this, the buyer was comfortable that, as long as the practice maintained a quality doctor-patient service level and got the patients in and out on a timely basis, there was reasonable certainly the revenue was sustainable.

To prove revenue sustainability, you may just need a camera. I once worked with a client who owned a profitable durable medical equipment business that sold wheelchairs, walkers, CPAP machines, and other such products. Since it was a retail business, we had no way to *prove* the business would continue to drive revenue. But one day I had the idea of taking an aerial photograph of the client's business because it was directly across the street from a massive hospital and a physicians' office complex. Of course, the buyer didn't need my visual to understand the point that proximity alone would likely imply revenue sustainability, but we had fun showing that picture, and it certainly helped make our point. People needing durable medical equipment were always going to be nearby.

You can also demonstrate sustainability through the testimony of customers. Back in my corporate days with Salem Communications, I studied the acquisition of a company that seemed to be a perfect fit for our strategy. To help understand the business, I asked the seller for a few references from his customers. After three or four calls with satisfied customers I quickly figured out that this seller had a great product. Once it was better marketed (which we could do), I knew the business had tremendous upside.

Thus, sustainability is in the eye of the buyer. Facebook sells advertising, which is often considered a lumpy revenue model. But one of the reasons Facebook has a ridiculously high valuation is that investors understand Facebook users are deeply committed to the site, visiting an average of nine times a day for sixty seconds or longer. In the eyes of Facebook shareholders, this is evidence of a sustainable revenue stream. Yes, contracted revenue is the purest evidence of sustainable revenue (per John Warrillow), but contracts will not be common in most business situations. You have to find creative ways to demonstrate that your revenue will be there after you are gone.

However, there is an occasional downside to the principle of sustainability. I have seen situations in which a business had a wonderfully sustainable revenue stream, but no growth potential embedded in the business.

I once worked with a very sharp woman who owned a successful daycare. She charged premium rates because she and her dedicated staff provided a premium level of care and support to the community's children. Her facility was licensed for 160 children and she rarely had a vacancy.

As we marketed her business, we had no problem proving revenue sustainability. Revenue was not going away. But we couldn't make much of a case for revenue growth potential because she was near her licensed capacity of 160 children. Maybe a buyer could raise rates, but my client was already charging a premium. So we ended up pricing her business on a modest multiple because, while the revenue was certainly sustainable, there was minimal upside for a buyer.

ONE FINAL THOUGHT about sustainability: revenue that looks sustainable may not be. My friend Derek started his business twenty years ago, and it's close to having $1 billion in annual revenue—not a bad start. Derek has made several acquisitions over the years, and he's always made sure the target acquisition's revenue was not tied to one or two salespeople.

"I will likely steer clear of a company that has 30 percent or more of its revenue tied to one salesperson, no matter how good the company might otherwise look," Derek told me.

Derek knows that sustainability of revenue takes on many forms, and *lack* of sustainability can be caused by many factors. That's why smart buyers will not take your company's financial information at face value. They will look under the hood: examine the sources of revenue, the categories of your customers, and how the revenue was brought to the company. Prove to your potential buyers that your revenue is predictable and sustainable, and you'll be irresistible.

But you can't make this case without reliable financials, which is the subject of our next chapter.

RELIABLE FINANCIAL STATEMENTS

I am usually not all that keen to drive four hours for a client meeting. But after my first call with David, I couldn't wait to meet him at his East Tennessee office. When he called to ask for help selling his company, he described his business and its successful fifteen-year history. David said he didn't want to sell, but his wife had been offered a professorship at the University of Illinois, an opportunity she could not pass up. David had no choice but to sell his business.

On the drive over I had plenty of time to think about what David said during our first call. Based on what he told me, I thought the business might sell for $4 to $5 million. In fact, I already had in mind a number of potential buyers that would likely be interested in the business. But I needed to see it for myself before I accepted the engagement.

My first clue there might be a problem was David's messy office. And when I say messy, I mean *messy*. After a few minutes of conversation, I asked to see his current financial statement, a standard question during my first visit with a prospective client. "There it is," he said, pointing to a shoebox beside his desk. I'm not exaggerating; I saw a shoebox full of paper. I guess he noticed the surprised look on my face as he said, "I guess I'm not too good with record keeping."

Suffice it to say, I could not help David sell his business. He didn't keep financial records for the business. He said he did his tax returns loosely based on his bank statements. I didn't get the sense David was running a tax scam, but he was beyond sloppy with his inattention to basic financial disciplines of running a business. Because of inattention and laziness, when David moved to Illinois he had no choice but to shut down what could have been a salable business. With decent financial statements, he could have made millions.

RELIABLE FINANCIALS: A MAKE-OR-BREAK FACTOR

Here's the understatement of the book: reliable financial records matter to buyers. Moreover, the better your financial records, the more you will get for your business. I tell business owners all the time that maintaining quality financials should not be considered an expense—it is an investment in making the company irresistible when it comes time to sell it.

Reliable financial records matter to buyers.

So, what do I mean when I say "reliable financial statements"? Simply put, the business must maintain an income statement and balance sheet consistent with basic principles of accounting standards, and those financials must sync with the business's bank statements and tax returns. All of these financial records must be in order for a buyer to feel secure about the stability of the business.

As noted in chapter 3, the business valuation process starts with the income statement (oftentimes referred to as the profit and loss statement, or P&L). I like to look at P&Ls for the past four years to get a snapshot of the company's revenue growth, gross margin, and overall profitability. I then look at the current balance sheet, along with the end-of-year balance sheets for the past four years. The current balance sheet gives me a snapshot of the company's financial health and its ability to fund its future, while prior years' balance sheets give me a snapshot of how the business has funded its operation. Having done this for a long time, a cursory review of these financials gives me a basic handle on how to think about the company's prospects when going to market.

Having said that, these financial statements are only as good as the inputs used to create them. As the old saying goes, garbage in, garbage out. So how do buyers know when they are looking at reliable financial statements? In my twenty-plus years of business transaction work, I have seen nearly every kind of financial statement available (even David's shoebox), but the most common types are audited, reviewed, and compiled. The differences come down to who does the analysis and the depth of that analysis.

AUDITED FINANCIALS

In a perfect world, every business owner would have financial statements annually audited by a certified public accountant (CPA). An audit is the highest level of assurance by an independent third-party CPA—meaning, not the CPA who works in-house for you, or the outside accountant who does your taxes. When you have an audit of your business, the conclusion you want to hear is that your financial statements are "free from material misstatement." This means the financial statement is accurate and consistent with generally acceptable principles of accounting practice (GAAP). The CPA will perform various procedures to obtain "reasonable assurance" the financial statements are free from material misstatement. The CPA is required to obtain an understanding of the business's internal control and assess fraud risk. The CPA is also required to corroborate the amounts and disclosures included in the financial statements by obtaining evidence through inquiry, physical inspection, observation, third-party confirmations, examination, analytical procedures, and other procedures. After this detailed analysis, the CPA will issue a formal opinion on whether the financial statements are presented fairly in all material aspects in accordance with applicable financial reporting standards. Also, the CPA is required to report any significant or material weaknesses in the system of internal controls identified during the audit. If the audit reveals internal control weaknesses, they should be addressed (fixed) before putting the business on the market.

If you are thinking this process sounds expensive, you would be right. But when taking your company to market, the highest quality financial records definitely work to your benefit. You know what a potential buyer thinks when you hand them your financial audit? They will assume you have nothing to hide and there will likely be no problems in the business operations. Remember the basic principle to which we return time and again throughout this book: the elimination of risk/uncertainty has positive implications on the value of the business.

REVIEWED FINANCIALS

Most businesses with less than $20 million annual revenue will not have audited financials. Owners generally believe they cannot cost-justify an audit. While that might ultimately be shortsighted, there is a lower level of financial scrutiny that will help a business owner when it is time to sell the company: reviewed financials.

In a review engagement, the CPA is required to understand the accounting principles and practices generally used in the industry in which the business operates. The CPA is also required to obtain sufficient knowledge about the business to identify areas in the financial statements where it is more likely that material misstatements may arise.

A financial review is substantially narrower in scope than an audit. A review does not require a deep dive into the business's internal control system, assessing fraud risk, testing accounting records through inspection, examining source documents, or other procedures ordinarily performed in an audit. For a financial review, the CPA will issue a report that includes, if necessary, a recommendation to make modifications to the financial statements to bring them into compliance with generally accepted accounting practices.

I encourage business owners with annual revenues of $3 million or more to have their financials reviewed each year. Even if taking the business to market is not on the owner's radar, having an annual financial review by a CPA will give the business owner a higher level of comfort as to the financial soundness of their business.

You want to avoid what happened to Doug. He retained me to sell his business and we entered serious negotiations with a Chicago-based private equity firm. Discussions were moving along nicely when the potential buyer asked for reviewed financials. Doug did not have reviewed financials, so we engaged an independent CPA—not the same CPA that did his tax work. When the report came back, it noted that Doug had not properly booked an equity grant to a key employee, so the financial statement had to be restated. That restatement ended up showing the business making less money in the prior two years. It was not an issue of fraud on Doug's part, it was just that he had not properly recorded the equity grant. However, as a result of this restatement, the business was worth a bit less in the eyes of the buyer. We were never able to close the valuation gap this created, and the deal did not get done. Had Doug known about this in advance, we would have presented the information differently;

we would have noted it as a non-cash adjustment and, likely, the private equity buyer would have been fine with it. But this snafu demonstrates a core principle when it comes to quality financials: you don't want to find accounting mistakes *during* the buyer's due diligence review. Once a buyer sees one mistake, the natural instinct is to assume there might be other mistakes, and, under those conditions, it's hard to make your business irresistible. The benefit of having financials reviewed—which is usually about 40 percent of the cost of an audit—is well worth the cost. Again, it's an investment in creating an irresistible business.

COMPILED FINANCIAL STATEMENTS

Most of the businesses I see have neither audited nor reviewed financials, but instead rely on what is called a compiled financial statement. This is when a third party takes financial records the business owner provides, and arranges that information into an understandable format. This third party might be the business's in-house accounting manager, or perhaps it will be the CPA who does tax returns for the business. But whoever does the report makes no statement regarding the accuracy or completeness of the report. More times than not, the financial data provided to the third party will come from some kind of accounting software (QuickBooks, NetBooks, Sage, etc.). But I have seen situations when the third party preparing the report is simply given a check register, and from that they can compile a reasonably accurate set of financial records.

WHAT'S THE POINT?

Reliable financial statements (income statement and balance sheet) get the owner to first base when it comes to selling the business. During the course of due diligence (which will be covered in greater detail in chapter 13), the buyer will also evaluate tax returns and bank statements to make sure all three forms of financial data (financial statements, tax returns and bank statements) are in sync.

I was once evaluating a company I was interested in buying. As I dug into the financial details, I could find no paper trail for the company's entertainment spending. There was a monthly cash withdrawal in roughly the same amount as entertainment, so I surmised those two were somehow linked. I asked the business broker to explain it, and he seemed clueless (whether intentionally or otherwise), so I asked the business owner. He hemmed and hawed a while but finally admitted he needed cash to entertain. As I got further into the conversation, he explained the cash withdrawals were used as gifts to customers' purchasing agents (to put it another way, bribes). Suffice it to say, I walked away right then and there. I didn't want to be near a business owner who was unscrupulous and likely breaking the law.

But beyond not doing business with crooks, the lesson I learned that day was the importance of carefully evaluating and reconciling financial statements, bank statements, and tax returns. It's amazing what you can learn when you sync the data.

Once I know we are working with reliable financial statements, I prepare an EBITDA report. This is a significant step that every buyer will require; as discussed in chapter 3, EBITDA is generally considered a good proxy for the company's cash flow (not to be confused with a cash flow statement, which will be discussed later). The financial statement we looked at in chapter 3 demonstrates the before and after of this process.

	2013	2014	2015	2016	2017	2018
Revenue	4,750	6,055	5,925	7,000	7,700	8,500
Cost of Goods Sold	(2,425)	(3,225)	(3,145)	(3,700)	(4,000)	(4,400)
Gross Profit	2,325	2,830	2,780	3,300	3,700	4,100
Operating Expense	(1,625)	(1,689)	(1,745)	(1,975)	(2,215)	(2,400)
Net Operating Income	700	1,141	1,035	1,325	1,485	1,700
Add Backs						
Depreciation	750	525	425	500	500	500
Interest	30	45	48	50	50	50
EBITDA	1,480	1,711	1,508	1,875	2,035	2,250
Adjustments						
One-time Extraordinary Expense	0	35	0	12	0	0
Owner Discretionary Expenses	9	9	6	12	12	12
Management Replacement	(135)	(135)	(150)	(150)	(160)	(160)
Adjusted EBITDA	1,354	1,620	1,364	1,749	1,887	2,102

EVALUATING ADD-BACK ADJUSTMENTS

Once we have determined EBITDA, we make additional adjustments in one of three categories: one-time/non-repeatable expenses, owner-discretionary expenses, and management replacement expenses. These adjustments then give us Adjusted EBITDA.

One-time/non-repeatable adjustments are expenses not part of the normal operating profile of the business. Let's say a business has a legal expense to settle a matter in litigation. Or maybe the company paid moving expenses to bring a key employee across country. These are legitimate expenses reflected on the company's income statement in the year they were paid, but they are one-time expenses, not likely to be repeated year in/year out. These kinds of expenses can be added back to EBITDA because they are not considered a normal part of business operations. And remember, the higher the Adjusted EBITDA, the greater the valuation.

A second category of add-backs is owner-discretionary expenses. These are expenses the owner passes through the company that are not considered a necessary and ordinary part of business operations. Say, for example, a business owner considers the cost of his football tickets as a business expense that shows up on the business income statement. That expense would be allowed as an add-back because football tickets are not required for the operation of a business (unless those tickets were used to entertain customers, key employees, etc.). Other examples of owner-discretionary expenses not required in the ordinary course of business would be a car for a spouse or child, first-class tickets to a business conference, or an extraordinary bonus taken by the owner.

The final category of add-backs is the cost to replace management when the owner is gone. I worked with a building supply company owner whose wife handled the company's accounting. The company had an EBITDA of about $500,000. The owner paid himself a salary of $80,000, and his wife a salary of $45,000. Both of these roles were vital to the healthy operation of the business, so we needed to ensure the appropriate cost to replace them was carried into the EBITDA adjustment. We studied the approximate cost to employ a general manager (GM) for the business and concluded that a salary of $80,000 was about the right number, so we made no adjustment for the GM salary. We also studied the approximate cost to employ an operations and financial manager to handle the functions the wife was performing, and we concluded the cost for that job was $60,000. Since she was being paid just $45,000, we had a *negative* add-back of $15,000.

Once the buyer and seller agree on the adjustments, that Adjusted EBITDA becomes the benchmark upon which valuation is determined. Similar adjustments can be made to a company's balance sheet, but in most cases, those adjustments are not material to understanding the capital structure of the business.

OTHER FINANCIAL STATEMENTS

Audited or reviewed financial statements and an Adjusted EBITDA statement are your starting points. But there are two other financial reports most buyers will want to see. In most transactions, the seller does not create these reports in advance, but instead has them prepared during the due diligence process. However, if you have the following statements prepared for prospective buyers in advance of their asking, you will be telegraphing your confidence in your business, making it more irresistible.

Remember what we said in chapter 3: all buyers really care about is a business's future cash-generating potential. Therefore, a buyer is going to ask for or create a statement of cash flows (also known as the flow-of-funds statement). This statement shows cash generated and cash used for a given period in three categories: operations, investments, and financing. The data for this report comes from the company's income statement and balance sheet. When buyers look at a cash flow statement, they are comparing cash from operating activities relative to the company's reported net income. If the cash from operating activities is consistently greater than net income, the company's net income—or earnings—is said to be of high quality, hence contributing to irresistibility. If a company is consistently generating more cash than it is using, the company will be able to invest in growth, increase its dividend, reduce debt, or make an acquisition. On the other hand, if the cash from operating activities is less than net income, it will raise a red flag because reported net income is not turning into cash.

So let's summarize what we know so far: a quality income statement and balance sheet gets you to the plate, a credible Adjusted EBITDA statement gets you to first base, and a statement of cash flows will put you firmly on second base. But if you really want to impress that buyer and hit it out of the park, prepare in advance a changes-in-working-capital statement, also referred to as a sources and uses of cash report.

Admittedly, this report is not easy to prepare. But, it's hard to get a deal done if the parties do not have a common perspective on the sources and uses of cash. For larger deals, say over $5 million, the buyer (and/or the buyer's lender) will require this report during due diligence. But, just like the statement of cash flows, if you can provide a sources and uses of cash flow report prior to in-depth discussions with potential buyers, you will greatly increase the chance of hitting your home run.

The importance of reliable financial statements cannot be overstated. It's not hyperbole to say a business without reliable financial statements cannot be sold for anything more than asset value.

EARLY IN MY CAREER I had another "shoebox client" who drove this point home. The business owner had been diagnosed with stomach cancer. Amazingly, he still looked good and seemed to be reasonably active in his business. But he knew he was on borrowed time and would have to sell the company eventually, so he called me.

Having reviewed scores—maybe hundreds—of companies, I don't fall in love all that often. But I *loved* this company, and I saw a huge opportunity for growth. In fact, after my first meeting with the owner, I came home and told my wife I would consider buying it. The owner had a reasonable valuation expectation of $3 million, based on his representation that the business was generating about $1 million per year in net operating income. But, in my second meeting with him, I learned he didn't keep financial records of any kind. He didn't even reconcile his bank statements when preparing tax returns. Most of his revenue and expenses were handled in cash, so the bank statements wouldn't offer an accurate picture of the business results anyway. He said he made up estimates every year for his tax returns. Amazingly, he had never been audited by the IRS (why, I'll never know). Once I saw the looseness of the operation, I knew I didn't want to buy it or be engaged to sell it.

Two years later, I ran into his son at a high school football game. He told me his dad passed away six months earlier, and he was in the process of selling the business's assets (equipment and land). He said he was hoping to get $150,000.

I have started and ended this chapter with extreme stories, but the principles are universal. Reliable financials take time and money, but when it's your time at the plate, reliable financial statements are often the difference between an embarrassing strikeout or a home run.

CHAPTER

9

DEMONSTRABLE SCALABILITY

What makes one business worth three times revenue and a similar business worth three times EBITDA? My client, Roger, was perturbed to learn his business was worth far less than the business recently sold by his close friend, Mike. Roger and Mike were in the same Entrepreneur's Organization (EO) forum. After Mike told Roger and his other forum members he sold his software company for three times revenue, Roger called me to say he was ready to sell his software company.

So why would I tell Roger his company was worth three times EBITDA, knowing Mike's business had just sold for three times revenue? The simple answer: *scalability*.

Scalability is a word that reminds me of a famous statement of US Supreme Court Justice Potter Stewart, who wrote the Court's decision for the landmark 1964 obscenity case, *Jacob Ellis v. Ohio*. The issue in that case was defining the fine line between obscenity and free speech. Making a reference to pornography, Justice Stewart wrote, "I know it when I see it." Stewart was making the point that it's hard to define obscenity, but when you see something obscene, you immediately recognize it as obscene. He was saying it's not a word you can define, it just is what it is.

That's how some people mistakenly feel about scalability. Business people throw around the word *scalable*, but very few understand what it really means. So, as a starting point, let me clear up a common misunderstanding: scale does not just mean *growth*. Scalability means *incrementally profitable growth*, which is another way of saying the next dollar of revenue is more profitable than the last dollar of revenue.

Simply said, scalability is when the rate of profit growth is faster than the rate of revenue growth. This phenomenon is what makes technology companies like Mike's so attractive. His company develops software for construction managers to better control on-site product costs. When you are building an eighty-story office building, controlling product costs is a very big deal, and the market for his software is global.

Mike invested $3.5 million to develop the software. After a couple years of market testing to find the right price point and marketing strategy, the software hit its stride in 2014, and the company has been on an annual growth curve of 30 percent.

The software needs to be updated and improved as technology progresses, but that's not a big expense. So Mike's only meaningful direct costs are those required to sell the product. He has three full-time salespeople who travel throughout the United States, and he uses an independent rep firm for exposure in Europe.

The cost of sales for Mike's company is about 25 percent of revenue. Since there are no other product development costs, the product has a gross margin of 75 percent. The buyer looked at Mike's company and saw its potential to reach customers in South Africa, South America, and Asia. So, the buyer saw untapped market potential, no new cost to develop the product, and a business model that demonstrates a terrific gross margin. Each new dollar of revenue will have a gross margin of at least 75 percent. As revenue grows, the cost of sales will likely go down as a percent of revenue. That is what a buyer would call a scalable business!

Now, Roger also has a software business, although he has a completely different business model. He writes customized software for the food service industry. While he uses the same basic architecture for each client, his team customizes the software based on the specific needs of each client. Each client need is configured, analyzed, and costed out before they even start the customization. He has the fixed costs to keep developers on staff, and, of course, he has the cost of a sales and marketing team. Roger is lucky to get 15 percent net profit margin on each sale. While potential buyers for Roger's company can see growth opportunity, they will probably not see a way to dramatically improve profit margins on that growth. While Roger's company still has a value of about five times EBITDA, his business doesn't scale, so he will not have the home run that Mike had.

I learned my lesson on the importance of scalability early in my career as a business broker. I had a client whose company provided consulting services for the hospital industry. They helped hospital accounting departments improve their billing practices. It was a profitable business: about 18 percent of every dollar of revenue dropped to the bottom line. My client, the owner, wasn't working in the business anymore. He had taken a job at the YMCA as its senior adult activities coordinator. He decided to sell his business when he realized his regular absence might eventually make some of his employees vulnerable to competitive offers. He summarized his decision this way: "I have no business without my key employees, so I better sell it while I can."

Given the stable revenue and strong profit margins in the business, I valued it at five times the most recent year's EBITDA (remember, this was early in my career.) I talked with buyers for more than six months, and the best offer we received was three times EBITDA. We eventually sold the business to a company in Delaware that had a similar consulting practice. During that negotiation, the buyer taught me an important lesson about scalability. He explained that, while my client's business was profitable and likely to stay profitable for the foreseeable future, if additional dollars were poured into fueling the growth of the business, the business would not improve its profit margin. The way he said it was, "The 18 percent profit margin is baked into the business model." He drew it out for me on a white board in his office. Each consultant can bill a maximum of 135 hours per month. You can't get more hours out of human capital, so the only way to grow revenue is to add new consultants, whose productivity is limited to 135 hours per month. To add new consultants, the business has to go through the process of finding, training, and getting the new hires up to speed. While adding new revenue via new consultants might increase the total profitability of the company, and that's certainly good, it doesn't improve the profit margin. In other words, the 18 percent profit margin was about the best the business could do. The business doesn't scale, and that's why knowledgeable buyers could not pay more than three times EBITDA for the consulting practice. This was a painful lesson for my client and me: people-intensive businesses are usually not scalable.

FINDING SCALABILITY

As we have covered many times before, buyers buy for future cash flow. If they don't see a future for incremental profitable growth in your company, your valuation cannot be maximized, and you are not likely to get that home run deal.

> **Buyers buy for future cash flow, and if they don't see a future for incremental profitable growth in your company, valuation cannot be maximized, and you are not likely to get that home run deal.**

That's why I advise business owners to look closely at their business model before they put their business on the market, and look for ways to make their business model scalable.

Let's assume you own a software business and create mobile apps on a time-and-materials basis for clients. Though not a scalable business, this can indeed be a profitable business model if you have a regular flow of clients that need new apps. But what if you converted some of your app development talent to developing your *own* apps? That way, you would have scalable revenue-generating products since selling apps has essentially no cost; as you grow revenue, the business would be incrementally more profitable.

Admittedly, my examples to this point have been technology-oriented companies, but the principle of scalability should apply to any business. Although it's an "old media" business, I love the sub-scription magazine business; this business model was scalable before scalability was cool. I once ran a magazine for devotees of southern gospel music. We had approximately eighty thousand subscribers, each paying $25 per year. When you include advertising, our total revenue was about $3 million per year, or $250,000 per month. We spent about $20,000 per month to produce the physical product with editorial and graphics. Salaries for our ad sales and subscrip-tion marketing team came to approximately $55,000 per month. It cost about $1.25 per month to print and mail each magazine, so our variable cost per month was approximately $120,000. So, our monthly net profit was: $250,000 (revenue) - $20,000 (fixed editorial/graphics) - $120,000 (variable print/mail cost) - $55,000 (salaries) = $55,000 (monthly profit).

Pretty cool, huh?

But here's why I *really* loved that magazine business. Every sub-scription brought in $25 per year, or $2.08 per month. The cost to print and mail one copy was $1.25, but, if we printed more magazines, our cost per copy was less than $1.25. Moreover, as we grew revenue, we had *zero* growth in fixed costs such as editorial, graphics, ad sales, and subscription marketing. Hence, every new dollar of subscription revenue was more profitable than the last. Of course, today the internet has eaten into the profitability of magazines since so much content is now available for free online. While demand for printed magazines is obviously not what it once was, subscription magazines demonstrate the beauty of scalability in a non-technology based business model.

Buyers of businesses love—and I mean *love*—businesses that can scale. A few months before this book was written, the company Blue Apron went public at a valuation near $2 billion. The young company's EBITDA is still negative, although trends show it moving toward profitability within a few more months. But how do you get a two billion valuation when you are losing money? Show scalability. The market is making the assumption that as Blue Apron continues to grow, its cost of customer acquisition will go down, which will improve operating margins (profitability). Only in the world of public markets can you get away with a completely insane valuation based on how you expect a new business to perform, but Blue Apron proves the point that if you can demonstrate scalability, your time at bat will be far more exciting.

Now that we know what scalability is (incrementally profitable growth), the obvious question is how do you get there?

Take a lesson from Verne, an enterprising ophthalmologist, who many years ago saw the promise of the coming wave of LASIK surgery clinics. He opened three clinics within two years and was soon being courted by private equity investors who wanted to fund his growth and open new clinics. With the help of that private equity investment,

Verne grew the business from three clinics to thirty clinics in just four years.

I heard Verne share the secret of his success at a conference I attended. The reason he was able to grow that quickly was the quality of systems used in the first three clinics. When that private equity investment came in, he didn't have to figure out his growth model. His team had developed systems for doing everything. Once the private equity firm had funded the growth of the clinics, the clinics had everything in place to grow incrementally more profitable. Each new dollar of revenue was incrementally more profitable than the last.

Scaled growth is easier said than done, but, when it's done, it's a beautiful thing and makes your business darn near irresistible.

CHAPTER

10

UNIQUE MARKET POSITION

When I was helping make acquisitions on behalf of the nation's preeminent Christian media company, we were looking for businesses that sold products or services of interest to the Christian audience on our 100-plus radio stations. Many opportunities came our way, but most did not meet our discriminating quality standards. One day we heard about a company with a distinctive market position. This company provided print-on-demand publishing services for authors of books with Christian-oriented content. Wow, what a perfect fit for us! Via our radio stations, we had an audience of tens of thousands of people committed to Christian content, and here was a business that sold a quality service specifically targeting that audience.

The founder of that company told me he had been repeatedly advised to broaden his service offerings beyond the Christian audience. After all, the service his company provided was relevant to any book genre. But the owner—who was a very smart guy— wanted to keep his business focused on this one target, the Christian audience. He built a distinctive brand presence that no other print-on-demand publisher could penetrate. From our perspective as buyers, his company's unique market position made his company irresistible. Moreover, as a strategic buyer, we paid more for the company than what he might have gotten from a financial or individual buyer. When he sold the business to us, he hit it out of the park.

What makes your company truly unique has to be premised on something real and tangible, not just marketing. For example, the concept of "secret sauce" was made famous in the 1960s by the McDonald's Corporation. In an effort to distinguish their core product, the Big Mac, the company often referred to its "secret sauce." For all I know, the secret sauce was just a simple mixture of mayonnaise and spices—but it was unique. It didn't have to be patented; it was just different. And you have to admit, this secret sauce made the Big Mac taste different from the cheeseburgers at Hardee's, Burger King, or your local diner.

Your secret sauce—your unique market position—is what makes your company genuinely stand out from your competitors. But here's a warning, when talking about your company being unique or distinctive, you have to go beyond generic qualities like great customer service or low prices. Those features are starting points necessary to even be in business today, but they aren't what make your company truly special.

I'm also not referring to snappy sloganeering. Nike's slogan, "Just Do It," is memorable and makes for great advertising, but it says nothing genuine about the company's products or services. And although I am a big fan of BMW cars and have been driving one for years, their slogan, "The Ultimate Driving Machine," implies nothing about why I should buy one. It's just a tagline that has nothing to do with what actually makes the company or their products special.

A buyer wants to know what makes your company distinctive, or truly special. How does your company stand out amongst your competitors? Not in fancy words or overused bromides, but what actually makes your company different, unique, and special? Maybe it's an exclusive supplier contract, a proprietary process, or a value-added component. Thirty years ago, the renowned Harvard Business School professor Michael Porter published *Competitive Advantage,* a groundbreaking book on the topic of creating and sustaining superior business performance.[3] His 700-page tome can be reduced to one theme: be the best at something.

I have a client in the restaurant business, and he says the reason he can sell pretzel appetizers for $11.00 is the quality of flour they use. This flour obviously costs more than all-purpose flour used by other restaurants. But once my friend's chef figured out their recipe with this unique flour, he had a competitive advantage over other restaurants that sold pretzel appetizers.

Now, being the *best* is a good thing, but being the *only* is better. If you can say, "We are the *only* company that does *X, Y, Z,*" then you are on the right track to proving your company has a unique market position. I once handled the sale of a company that provided continuing medical education seminars for allied healthcare professionals. It was a well-run company and the customers loved the high-quality seminars. But one thing that caught the attention of the private equity buyer: my client's company was the only company that offered allied healthcare seminars in all fifty states. It was not a catchy slogan, it was a reality, and it made the company special.

I love the distinctive market position taken by Harry's, the company that sells shaving products. Perhaps you're familiar with its commercials for shaving blades. They say the company is so focused on quality that it bought the German factory where the blades are manufactured. Now, I am not sure that owning a factory actually makes shaving blades better than anybody else's, but owning a

---

3   Michael E. Porter, *The Competitive Advantage: Creating and Sustaining Superior Performance (with a new introduction),* New York: Free Press, 2008.

manufacturing plant in Germany is a genuinely distinctive market position. Compare that with another major player in the shaving business, Gillette: "The best a man can get." Uh? What does that mean? Any rational human hears that as nothing more than a slogan created by the marketing department. There's nothing *real* about it.

Figure out how to finish this statement, "We are the *only* company that…" Own it, deliver on it, and stay with it. When it comes time to sell your company, buyers will find your "only" irresistible. Having said that, don't think your specialness has to be defined in your marketing materials. It might be how you operate business. I once represented a company that had a basic service offering. What it did wasn't all that special, but it had very strong economics: revenue of $20 million per year with 15 percent profits—a money making machine. However, I could not get private equity investors interested in the deal, even though the economics were very strong. It took me a while to finally figure out what was going on. When private equity investors looked at this company, they did not see anything special about it. In fact, one private equity professional admitted that he liked the company, but there was nothing he could brag about in his firm's partner meeting.

Initially, his answer struck me as shallow. I would have thought that great economics alone would be sufficient bragging rights. But he made it clear we'd never get to first base on this deal without finding a special angle. I went back and gave my client this feedback, and he was similarly frustrated. We began to think about whether there was anything truly special we could claim. It wasn't immediately obvious, but as we talked, we realized the reason he could drive a dependable $20 million per year revenue stream was the creative way he structured his sales force. This wasn't immediately obvious to him because he was so close to it, and the sales team structure was how he had been doing business for years. But when we looked at this structure relative to his competitors, we realized he did indeed have a special angle that made the company unique.

About two weeks after this conversation, my client told me he decided to not sell the company. I never told him this—he's likely to read it for the first time in this book—but I think his coming to grips with a sense of "specialness" about his company reinvigorated him for another few years of ownership.

Specialness does not necessarily have to translate to being exciting. I was once retained on a consulting basis to help a seven-person law firm go through the process of being sold. While I don't practice law anymore, I am proud of my membership in the Missouri Bar Association, and I reflect fondly on my days in a courtroom. But, I have to admit, selling a law firm is not the most exciting thing I've ever done. Yeah, it's basically true: lawyers and the practice of law can be boring. Many lawyers and practices are essentially the same with very little to differentiate them. But the firm I was helping specialized in intellectual property law for songwriters and music publishers. From the outside, this firm looked like a garden-variety Nashville Music Row law firm, but then I learned this small team of seven lawyers had more articles published in intellectual property law journals than any law firm in the Southeast.

This credible and real distinctiveness helped in our discussions with major law firms in the Northeast that were looking to enter the music publishing market in Nashville.

Let me be clear: being special is not a requirement to sell your company, but it will help you sell your company for more than its basic economic value. A special angle increases value because it helps make your company irresistible.

I have a friend who works in human resources for a Fortune 100 company. He is responsible for filling the company's positions at the director level and above. In telling me how he evaluates candidates, he said if two candidates are otherwise equal in terms of background, experience, and personality, if one of the candidates has run a marathon, he will make that the basis of his hiring decision. My friend is not a runner, in fact, he isn't much of an athlete. But he said he believes running a marathon says something special about a person. Even a highly rational person like my friend recognizes how a *perception of specialness* can affect his decisions.

> **Being special is not a requirement to sell your company, but it will help you sell your company for more than its basic economic value. A special angle increases value because it helps make your company irresistible.**

The principle of specialness is important when selling a business because buyers will analyze your company every which way, then come to a rational, left-brain perspective regarding valuation. But what makes your company special will push that rational analysis into right brain, emotional territory, and when that happens, valuations go up. It's almost like a principle of nature, although hard to explain, yet evident in so many ways. When buyers see that your company has something truly special to differentiate it, they will find you simply irresistible.

OWNER INDEPENDENCE

It may seem like an oxymoron, but the less you are needed in your business, the more value you will see when you are ready to sell. The opposite is also true. If the business revolves around you, when you sell you have reduced your chance of hitting a home run.

I HAVE A GOOD FRIEND, Michael, who sold his company in 2002. The buyer knew Michael was key to making the business work, so, instead of cash at close, Michael agreed to keep working in the business and be paid over seven years. In year three, the buyer stopped paying, so Michael regained ownership of the company. "The day I took back control I was determined to not let that happen again," Michael told me. "I knew I couldn't be the center of the universe if I ever wanted to sell the business for cash at close." When Michael regained control over the business, he completely retooled how he managed it. He took himself out of the center of decision-making by creating systems and processes for his employees.

Here's the logic of this principle (in fact, you might even want to circle this statement): a buyer's worst fear is to buy a business and come to the office the next morning to realize the employees, customers, or suppliers have left after the owner announced the sale of the business. Perhaps the buyer's second worst fear is that after making the acquisition the employees are still there, but no one knows what to do! In either situation, the business relied too heavily on the owner, and once he or she was out of the picture, the business was at risk of falling apart.

Although these examples sound extreme, I've seen far too often businesses that are overly dependent on the owner. In these situations, unless the buyer is comfortable stepping into the seller's role on day one (which is unlikely), the seller is not going to hit a home run when the business is sold. In fact, if a business is too owner-dependent, that owner may never even get to first base when trying to sell it.

In his highly regarded book, *The E-Myth*, Michael Gerber urges entrepreneurs to work *on* their businesses, not *in* their businesses.[4] If the owner is working *in* the business, the business is probably overly dependent on him/her. In contrast, if the owner spends more time working *on* the business, there's a stronger likelihood the business can survive after the owner is gone. Take the case of Phillip, who owned a public relations agency that helped up-and-coming artists get exposure on country music radio. Artists paid a fee to Phillip's agency, and Phillip's staff of highly experienced publicists went to work to get radio exposure for their clients. Phillip's profit margins were insanely good; the bulk of his expenses were salaries for his staff, which were willing to work at below-market rates for the opportunity to work

---

4   Michael F. Gerber, *The E-Myth: Why Most Small Businesses Don't Work and What to Do about It*, New York: Harper & Row (HarperCollins), 1991.

from home. But coordinating a disconnected staff was a challenge, and Phillip was seldom off the phone jumping from one staff question to the next. Despite inefficiencies inherent in not having the staff together in one place, the clients were happy, and the radio stations they served loved having a steady pipeline of new music.

Phillip approached me about selling his agency because, like many entrepreneurs, he had a few new ideas he wanted to pursue. And although he never quite said it, Phillip seemed a bit bored and just ready to move on to something new. He told me he wanted $4 million for his agency. Based on his financials, that seemed feasible. But as I learned more about how his agency worked, I became concerned that too much of the business revolved around Phillip. He had been in the country music business since he graduated from college, and everyone in the industry knew him. His strong reputation bred a constant pipeline of new business. The question was, if Phillip ever left the agency, would this pipeline of new business continue to flow. Several companies were interested in buying the agency, but it never took more than fifteen minutes of conversation with Phillip to figure out how important he was to making the whole system run. Phillip was making great money, but he had not worked to create a method to develop new business that extended beyond his personal reputation. In Michael Gerber-speak, Phillip spent too much time working *in* the business, but not *on* the business. To maximize the value of the agency, Philip needed to work *on* developing revenue-generating processes that would work with or without him. As will be discussed in chapter 12, Phillip needed to develop a sustainable, post-Phillip revenue model. After all, who would buy the agency and not be terrified that its pipeline of new business would dry up once Phillip was gone?

Lack of owner independence is an epidemic in personal services businesses. For another example, take Rudy, who gave me a tour of his business that was unlike anything I had ever seen before (or hope to see again). You see, Rudy owned a funeral business. He and his wife—who worked in the business with him—were ready to retire and enjoy more time with their grandchildren. Now let me point out that Rudy was not your image of a typical funeral director. He had been one of the first male cheerleaders at his college, which made sense given his infectious, warm personality. As he showed me around his funeral home, I had trouble seeing how he could take on that quiet, somber image we expect from funeral directors. But Rudy's financials told the story of a successful business, and he was ready to sell and reap the rewards of many years of hard work.

But, like Phillip, Rudy *was* the business. Even though he would occasionally use part-time licensed funeral directors when he needed to leave town or had more work than he could handle, for all practical purposes, Rudy *was* the business. His name was on the door, and his reputation for quality service drove the referrals that kept him busy for over twenty years.

Similar to Phillip, Rudy had a capable support staff. But without him coming to work every day the business would suffer, and, in all likelihood, eventually collapse. His business was not owner independent. If Michael Gerber knew Rudy or Phillip, he would say they were prototypical examples of entrepreneurs working *in* the business, not *on* the business. When buyers look at businesses like these, they see the likelihood of the revenue stream evaporating after the sale. No matter how successful the business might be, the owner is not likely to hit a home run when it's time to sell.

TO SEE WHAT owner independence really looks like, consider Steve's situation. As a starting point, understand that Steve didn't know much about his business, but he knew how to manage people. He was a successful homebuilder, an entrepreneur to the core. Right after the recession of 2008, Steve was building a home for a plastic surgeon. In the course of the project, the surgeon made a passing comment to Steve that the practice where he worked was going through some challenges and might need to be sold. Ever the entrepreneur, Steve probed for more information and after lots of study he saw a way to acquire the plastic surgery practice. Suffice it to say, Steve didn't know a thing about the practice of medicine, but he did understand a thing or two about customer acquisition. He told me he bought the business knowing he could create a marketing system to keep new patients coming to the practice. Over time, his system generated a predictable revenue stream.

Steve was working on the business, certainly not in the business, the classic embodiment of owner independence. No prospective buyer looked at the business and ever worried about it faltering once Steve was out of the picture. Of course, given the nature of the business (medical services), Steve had no choice but to work on the business rather than in the business. But, the principle applies to any business owner who wants to eventually sell: remove yourself from the middle of business operations and work to develop systems, processes, and a culture that can function without you. If you do this, once you are ready to sell your business, you are significantly more likely to see the ball fly over the fence.

Here are a couple of questions a buyer will always ask to get at the heart of owner independence: who is the main interface with the best customers? If the answer is you, the owner, you have a problem. A buyer will likely also ask: who makes final decisions about capital spending and key hires? If the answer is not you, you will be in great shape when you are ready to sell your business.

MY FRIEND CODY once told me a funny story about how he hit a home run when selling his professional services business. When he decided to sell, he met with several potential buyers and found himself in the uncomfortable position of not having answers to many basic questions, because, as he put it, "I don't make all the decisions. That's why I put my team together." So, while Cody didn't know it at the time, his inability to answer all the questions was indicative that the business was not overly dependent on him.

A few weeks after these initial meetings, Cody was invited to visit the CEO of a company that seemed to be the perfect buyer. "I was scared as hell of making a fool of myself," Cody said, "so I took my executive team to the meeting. I figured I might look stupid for not knowing everything, but at least the CEO would get the answers he was looking for."

Well, you probably know how the story ends. Cody hit it out of the park when he sold his business, and now he spends a lot of time on his sailboat in the Bahamas. That company bought Cody's business in part because the CEO was so impressed with Cody's management team. "I didn't know it at the time,"

Cody told me, "but taking my team along was the clearest evidence I could provide that I wasn't critical to running the business. The CEO called me on my drive home to tell me how impressed he was with the team and that an offer would soon be on the table."

I tell this story about Cody to almost every business owner with whom I meet. His story is the most obvious example I've seen that demonstrates the value created when the business is not overly dependent on the owner. Cody started the business twelve years earlier, but instead of hiring a team of people to help him run his business, he managed the team that ran his business. And now Cody has a permanent tan as evidence of the wisdom of that decision.

And what about the friend to whom I referred at the start of this chapter, Michael? He was serious about not allowing the business to revolve around him the second time. He intentionally built a management team and put systems in place that allowed him to work on the business, not be the center of the business. A few years later, he sold the business for a fabulous amount of cash at close. Michael hit a home run.

A buyer will look at your business to see if it can operate without you. But the buyer will also need to see growth potential in your business. Is the story you tell about future growth believable? That's the final principle of irresistibility.

12

BELIEVABLE GROWTH STORY

"All this business needs to grow is more marketing." As Ron said this, I thought to myself, *Gee, I've heard that one a million times.*

Ron started his metal building manufacturing company in 1984, and it provided a nice living for him and his family. After his wife passed away in 2014, his daughter pushed him to sell the business and move closer to his grandkids in southern Texas. Pictures of his family were scattered throughout his office, so it was obvious his family was the center of his life.

When we first spoke, Ron asked the two questions I hear from every business owner during our first conversation: "How much is my business worth," and "How long will it take to sell it?"

I wanted to study Ron's financial history before giving him an answer, but it didn't take long to realize that selling the business might be a problem—well, at least selling it for the price he wanted. Ron's EBITDA was about $200,000 per year, but during the past three years revenue had plateaued while his cost of doing business was going up. In other words, the business was slightly less profitable year over year. While I felt comfortable I could find a buyer, I was reasonably certain his $1 million exit objective was not realistic. A buyer would see the business as a turnaround play, and not deserving of a high multiple.

Ron's situation is typical of many retiring baby-boomer business owners. With the passage of time, they have either taken their foot off the gas pedal or have seen their business affected by the slow-growth economy or outside competitive factors. In Ron's case, the business almost folded during the recession of 2008–2009. Fortunately, he held on through that stress, though it had taken almost seven years to get revenue back to where it was before the recession. However, during this period of long recovery, the cost of doing business had increased faster than revenue.

What Ron needed was a strategy to grow revenue. As we met over a catfish lunch at a local diner, I told Ron the business could be sold, but not for the price he wanted. He acknowledged that his best option might be to keep the business another couple of years to work on getting its valuation up to the point he wanted. That's when I asked him the million-dollar question (in this case, literally, his answer could be worth $1 million): "So, if you keep the business, what will you do to get it growing again?" And that's when he said, "All this business needs is more marketing."

There might have been a time when a business owner could just throw money at marketing and see the business grow. I have a long-time friend who owns a pharmacy in a small town. He told me there used to be a time when his revenue would go up or down based on the amount of advertising he bought during the Rush Limbaugh radio show. Unfortunately, the apparent simplicity of that growth strategy is not replicable for most business owners today given changes in how people now consume media.

Let's look at how advertising has changed since Ron started his business. His target customers are farmers within a 150-mile radius of his plant in north central Tennessee. During his first twenty years, Ron's marketing choices were fairly simple. He relied on local radio and direct mail to drive leads. Calls from potential customers came in on a toll-free line to the two sales representatives in his office. Occasionally, a potential customer would request a meeting before making a purchase, so Ron maintained a network of independent sales reps to do on-site visits. The process wasn't very complicated, and it grew to a $10 million business just before the 2008 recession. But, in the years since, everything changed for Ron. Quality labor was harder to find, and when he did find good employees, they wanted to be paid more. Getting overtime out of his labor force was like pulling teeth. The cost of steel had gone up, and the cost to transport it was more expensive. But the greatest complication for Ron was marketing. Direct mail had become prohibitively expensive. Local radio still worked somewhat, but it wasn't nearly as effective because farmers no longer relied on local radio for weather reports. Ron's other complication was keeping qualified and hard-working independent field reps. As he said to me that day at lunch, "Nobody wants to work on all-commission anymore."

So, in this ever-changing landscape, I asked Ron his plan to restart revenue growth. His answer of "more marketing" just didn't make sense. It might have been the right answer for 1989, or maybe even 1999, but for 2017 it was a recipe for throwing money away. I explained to Ron that without a believable story for growth, his business would not be irresistible, and he would not be in a position to sell his business for a premium. Ron's plan for growth—more marketing—was well intentioned based on what had worked in the past, but an increase in marketing is not a strategy for growth.

It's axiomatic that business buyers want and expect growth. That's how they get a financial return on their investment. So, without a strategy for growth, how likely is it somebody will want to buy your business? But as we learned with Ron's situation, the word "strategy" does not mean "more marketing." Coming up with an actual strategy requires an answer to two questions: (1) "How much do I invest?" and, (2) "What kind of return can I expect?" If you can answer those two questions, you have a believable growth story, and you're one step closer to hitting that home run when it's time to sell your business.

> **Without a strategy for growth, how likely is it somebody will want to buy your business?**

Let's get back to my friend who owns the small-town pharmacy. When he was an active buyer of commercial time on the Rush Limbaugh radio show, he owned one of the two pharmacies in his town. Today there are four independent pharmacies—and the local Wal-Mart has a large pharmacy. The new Kroger is also going to have a pharmacy. Needless to say, my friend has far more competition today than he had just five years ago. Customer development has not only gotten complicated, it's gotten more expensive and less effective, which is not exactly the combination one wants for a growing business. My pharmacist friend decided that his new definition of business success would be the absence of further decline, which means taking really good care of existing customers. However, I warned him that in the absence of a plan to grow the pharmacy business, he wasn't likely to see much value when he was ready to sell it.

Contrast that with a friend from college who recently sold his company to a German-based private equity group. In the early 1990s, my friend developed a software program to help architects manage their workflow. Through the years, he improved the software by adding functionality, speed, and reliability. About ten years after he launched the software, he saw the emergence of technology that would enable him to deliver the software via the internet instead of the original method of installing it by CD. My friend was ahead of the curve with the transition to cloud computing, but that was not the most compelling aspect of his business to the private equity firms that bid for his company.

My friend had developed a database of every architectural firm in North America, South America, Europe, and Australia. He had a process by which he contacted 10 percent of this potential market every year through a combination of e-mail, direct mail, and outbound sales calls. This strategy fostered an annual growth of 9 percent over four years. While he had an eight-figure annual revenue stream at the time he sold his company, he estimated he had only reached 12 percent of the potential market. See the point? His strategy for future growth was not just "more marketing," but turbo-charging the quantifiably-proven activities he had used to grow his business to that point. He was able to demonstrate that increased spending on these same activities would enable the business to reach more than 15 percent of the market every year and therefore produce faster growth. He had a believable growth strategy—a story for how to grow the business.

Simply said, a believable growth story goes like this (you might want to circle these next few lines): Here's what we have done in the past and here are the results it generated. We therefore know that doing X percent more of what we have done in the past will generate Y percent new business. Contrast that with the statement, "All I need to grow is more money in marketing." One statement is specific and measurable, while the other is general. Which would you believe?

Another angle from which to prove a believable growth strategy is demonstrating synergy between your company and a buyer's. Let's say you own an agency that sells property and casualty insurance. You do all the normal things to promote your agency, such as sponsoring a little league team, buying ads in the local newspaper, and sending direct mail to homeowners in your area. But you haven't cracked the code for demonstrating growth. So, while you don't yet have a believable growth story, you know that if you added new product lines you could sell more to your existing customers and likely even add new customers. In this example, your believable growth story might be to add a couple of salespeople focused on life insurance. But perhaps an even better growth story is what your business could generate if it was owned by an agency that specialized in life insurance. That buyer would love your growth story.

Your growth story could also center on making a strategic investment. I once helped a business owner develop a growth strategy as part of his plan to sell his company in five years. The company manufactured baked goods for school cafeterias, most of which were located within a 200-mile radius of his plant because delivering freshly baked goods was his point of differentiation. He called me for advice on buying a building in the Carolinas that could be converted to a second plant, from which he could dramatically broaden his market territory. We calculated the cost to buy the real estate, convert the building, equip the plant, and add staff. The total investment over a three-year period was going to be $18 million. My client calculated this investment would drive $8 to $10 million in new annual revenue within three years after the plant was open. In other words, he had a six-year window from his decision to build the plant to the point the decision would generate returns sufficient to justify the investment. It was a brilliant growth strategy, but six years was beyond the scope of his planning objectives. That's another way of saying he didn't want to be strung out for six years, even though he was confident the investment would pay off. He didn't want to abandon the plan, but he didn't want to go it alone. At that point we began conversations with strategic and financial buyers who were attracted to the opportunity in large part because he had a tangible and believable story for future growth.

Your business might not fall into any of these categories. You might not have a believable story for growth other than to keep doing what you are doing because it seems to be working. I don't want to discourage you. Your company might still be salable. But, when you find that buyer, or that buyer finds you, you're not likely to get an above-market premium for your company unless *your company* is part of the *buyer's* growth story.

TAKE, FOR EXAMPLE, when I was helping a business owner, James, sell his company early in my career. James needed to sell his business to relocate with his wife, who had just received a nice promotion with her corporate employer. Selling his business was going to be difficult; there wasn't much of a story to be told about growth. He provided a useful service and made enough money to pay himself a fairly decent salary, but I didn't see much upside that would be exciting to a buyer.

Additionally, knowing he had to sell didn't help us in the negotiation phase. Buyers ask why an owner is selling, and it's my policy to always tell the truth about everything—the buyer will find out the truth eventually, so you might as well be up front about it. Suffice it to say, we had little negotiating leverage, and there was no compelling growth story. We were getting offers just slightly above asset value. James was stuck. He didn't want to give his company away, but he knew his options and time were limited. He decided to hold on to the company and travel back and forth from his new home until he could figure out a solution. It proved to be a smart (lucky?) decision. About six months after he started this back-and-forth lifestyle, he learned that one of the big national players in his industry was looking to consolidate small, local service providers like him. James knew he could sell his company for a premium because his company played into the growth strategy of the buyer. Our task was to make a believable case for how his company would fit into the buyer's growth strategy.

Your growth story might just involve getting a bigger bucket. I once helped a client sell his tree-cutting business. About 25 percent of his business was regular maintenance for affluent residential customers, and the balance came from work resulting from damage done by unpredictable but frequent storms that cause nuisance tree collapses. My client could never reliably forecast revenue, but from years of experience he knew that spring thunderstorms and winter ice would always result in damaged and downed trees. He was particularly busy during those seasons.

But my client knew his experienced team of tree experts could take on more work. There were state contracts available for roadside tree removal, but those contracts required the company have a certain kind of bucket truck. That equipment cost $200,000, and most state contracts required two-truck crews, meaning the total cost to get into that new line of business was about $400,000. As part of the believable growth story for my client's otherwise stable business, we talked to prospective buyers about this new investment opportunity.

Your chances of selling your business are not very high if you cannot demonstrate the potential to grow your business. But if you can convert potential to a demonstrable, articulate plan for growth, you are likely to hit it out of the park when it's your time at the plate.

SECTION III

Getting Home Safely

You have prepared the right way, and your potential buyer finds your business irresistible. Well done—so far—but don't celebrate just yet. You still have to make it around all the bases.

The process of finding that right buyer to seeing the money hit your bank account can take months of hard work and anxious late nights. About 50 percent of transactions that get to the letter of intent (LOI) stage never close—an embarrassing strikeout at the plate. This happens for one of three reasons: (1) the prospective buyer learns something during due diligence that changes their mind, (2) the prospective buyer learns something that prompts them to try to renegotiate terms and the seller walks away, or (3) the seller develops remorse and backs out. Knowing these possibilities exist should help you to avoid them and complete your home run.

CHAPTER 13

THE MYSTERY OF DUE DILIGENCE

The 1993 World Series hung in the balance when Joe Carter came up to bat for the Toronto Blue Jays against Philadelphia Phillies pitcher Mitch Williams. It was the bottom of the ninth inning and Philadelphia was leading six to five. Carter pounded a series-winning three-run home run over the left field wall. The Toronto announcer, Tom Cheek, was overcome with emotion. As Carter rounded second base, Cheek excitedly said, "Touch 'em all, Joe. You'll never hit a bigger home run your whole life!"

This is considered one of the most famous home run calls in baseball's illustrious history. But when announcer Tom Cheek said that now-famous line, he was giving Carter advice that you, as a business owner, must also follow. When Carter hit the home run, fans and players stormed onto the field and pandemonium ensued, so Carter had to pay extra attention to make sure he touched all the bases. You see, even if you hit the baseball out of the park, the rules say you still have to run and touch all of the bases, or you will be called out at home plate.

Great advice, Tom Cheek! Carter could not celebrate his glorious result without first focusing on the task at hand, which was touching all the bases. Likewise, many business owners in the process of selling assume once there is a signed LOI (sometimes also called a terms sheet), they can relax, wade through some paperwork, and wait for closing. But, just like Joe Carter, business owners cannot lose focus as they complete the final steps of selling the business, and that final stage is called due diligence.

Pretty much the equivalent of a colonoscopy on your business, due diligence is the process by which the buyer evaluates your business from the outside in and the inside out. The point of due diligence is the buyer making sure everything the seller has represented about the business is true, and that the buyer will not find bombs waiting to go off after closing.

> **Pretty much the equivalent of a colonoscopy on your business, due diligence is the process by which the buyer evaluates your business from the outside in and the inside out.**

The buyer will evaluate your financial records to ensure that your accounting statements, tax statements, and bank statements are in sync. Noncompliance with generally accepted accounting procedures (GAAP) will come to light during due diligence. The buyer will evaluate the quality of your product, service, and/or systems. Lack of equipment maintenance will come to light during due diligence. Key customers on the verge of leaving will come to light during due diligence. Dissatisfied key employees or employees ready to retire will come to light during due diligence. Supplier or customer contracts that are not optimal will come to light during due diligence. Something you or your intermediary said during the marketing phase of the process that turns out to not be true will come to light during due diligence.

Get the picture? Due diligence is when it *all* comes to light, and when I say all, I mean all. Simply said, due diligence is the process for the buyer to make sure there are no skeletons in the closet of the business. I have a friend who does due diligence review for a living, and he describes it this way, "Due diligence is the process we go through to make sure the target company has no black holes that will swallow the buyer after closing."

You should be proactive during due diligence to help the buyer evaluate the good and the bad in your company. And here's why: your proactive involvement will help the process from LOI to closing go faster and smoother. On the other hand, if the seller is not helpful and attentive during the due diligence process, the buyer might become suspicious the seller is hiding something. That can lead to a deal collapsing altogether, or price and terms being renegotiated.

Due diligence starts after the parties sign an LOI. The LOI is a non-binding agreement executed by the buyer and seller to show they have reached a basic meeting of the minds on price and key terms, demonstrating their mutual willingness to start the process of spending money to get the deal closed. But understand that the time between the LOI and closing is precarious, and things tend to change.

The seller and buyer will initially be excited about the proposed transaction—the key word being *proposed*. Just as with a marriage proposal, things can go wrong between the proposal and the big event. I've seen deals fall apart because of changes in the business or regulatory environment, and I've even seen deals go south because of changes in political or economic conditions. Personal issues, such as death or divorce, may rear their ugly heads during this time as well. Anything that produces uncertainty for either party can cause a deal to not get done.

It's your job as the seller to keep your buyer excited and engaged. Stay in touch with the buyer. Keep focused on the bright, profitable, growth-filled future outlined in your marketing package. When you have fresh, good news to pass along about the business (a great sales month, a break-through new account, or a key new hire), make a call and talk it up. Like an attentive suitor, woo right up until the day of the wedding. Never take for granted the sale is a done deal until it's a done deal. Due diligence is a tricky process and it's likely to throw you a number of curve balls. Bart's story illustrates the danger.

I met Bart when we played together in a charity golf event. He told me he was going to be closing in two weeks on the sale of his family-owned business to a European-based buyer for $36 million. Bart was CEO, and he owned the company along with his older brother, and his younger sister. They were the second generation owners; their father and uncle had started the business in the early 1960s.

"Dad wanted it to be a family-owned business forever," Bart told me that day on the golf course, "but this offer was just too good to be true."

So imagine my surprise when I got a call from Bart a few weeks later: "Remember that deal I was telling you about that day we played golf, the one I said was too good to be true?"

"Of course," I replied. "I remember it well, because you told me about the golf trip to Ireland and Scotland you planned to take after the deal was closed. I take it something went wrong?"

Bart anticipated my obvious question and quickly said, "We backed out five days before the scheduled closing because the buyer wanted to renegotiate the price down based on a slow third quarter. All the way through due diligence the buyer had been nickel-and-diming us on everything, and we finally had to say, 'No more, we're done with you guys.' So now we need to decide if we go back on the market. Can you meet with the board and give us your perspective?"

So about a week later I found myself sitting in a boardroom at the head of a table with six people solemnly looking back at me. It felt more like a morgue than a conference room.

"What the hell do we do now?" asked the older gentleman sitting directly across the table from me. "You don't have to curse," said the woman sitting to my right.

That's how our meeting started.

The board was comprised of Bart, his brother, his sister, and their respective spouses. As I listened to them go back and forth, it was apparent there wasn't a consensus about next steps. As is often the case with family-only boards, they weren't entirely functional in the first place. But with the added trauma of the recent deal gone bad, they had almost ceased to function as a board. With the plan to sell the company now in the recycle bin, the board members found themselves at a critical juncture: they needed a consensus strategy going forward, but reaching that consensus was going to be difficult. The older brother and his wife were blaming Bart for the failure to get the deal closed, although from my perspective Bart was leading the company with integrity and a genuine desire to maximize value for all the shareholders.

Two weeks after my first meeting with the board, I presented my research, finding that they could sell the company for $42 to $45 million. I had to tell them they had been lucky to be dealing with a potential buyer who was greedy. While $36 million initially sounded like a great offer, it didn't represent full value for the company given what was going on in their industry. I explained to the board that several companies in their industry were making strategic acquisitions, and they'd likely be able to maximize the value of the company through a controlled auction. The first prospective buyer had blown it trying to squeeze every last dollar out of the deal.

I've seen this kind of thing happen during the due diligence stage. Buyers think they have an inside track on getting a deal done, so they get clever and try to push the seller as they near closing. Fortunately for Bart and his contentious siblings, the first buyer's greed during due diligence ultimately resulted in the family members splitting several more millions at closing.

When I sold my radio company, I got caught in a bind during due diligence because I told two key employees I was selling the company. I told them how being part of the buying company was going to be good for their careers, how much they would love the buyer, and so on. But after I told them this, the prospective buyer wanted to renegotiate a couple of key terms. I was caught between a rock and a hard place because I had convinced my employees that selling was in their best interests. If I did not sell, they might have been disappointed. Yet, by going through with the deal, I was going to get less than I thought when the deal was first proposed. Fortunately, there was a happy ending. Others are not so fortunate, as in the case of Martin.

"WHEN THE OFFER CAME IN at $15 million, I told them I needed to think about it. Three seconds later, I accepted." Martin rolled his eyes as he told me his story. "Stupid me for assuming they were serious, so now here I am, two years later, and no deal."

Martin had called to discuss his interest in selling his company. I didn't know until we met that day that he had already gone through this process with a potential buyer. But when I heard how it had turned out, his story sounded all too familiar.

"They called me out of the blue and said they were interested in expanding into the United States, and that my plant in Tennessee was the perfect place to start. It all made sense at the time, but I wasted a lot of time, energy, and money going through the due diligence process with those guys. I wish I'd known then what I know now."

I didn't want to hurt Martin's feelings; he felt bad enough already. So I gingerly said, "Gee, I wish you had called me earlier. I could have helped you."

Martin calmly replied, "Yes, I should have called you the second they put an offer on the table." He went on to explain that once he had accepted their offer and signed the LOI, the buyer sent in a team of accountants and engineers to review every detail of his operation. "I lost seventy days of productivity babysitting those guys," he said. "But I thought I was going to sell the company, so it seemed like a necessary evil." The fact that Martin never completed that deal is, unfortunately, quite common. It happens far too frequently when a business owner gets an unsolicited, too-good-to-be-true offer. Although the buyer was a credible company with resources to complete the deal, we now know the company was just on a fishing expedition. Looking back on it, it's obvious this "buyer" was going through this process with Martin before even finalizing their decision to enter the American market. Here's why I say that: after finishing the due diligence, which took almost three months, the company representatives told Martin that before a formal offer would be forthcoming they needed to run the idea by their board. Martin heard nothing for two months. The buyer's investment banker eventually called to say the buyer couldn't complete the deal because exchange rates had affected the buyer's operating results in Europe. It was a lame excuse, revealing that acquiring Martin's company had not been a strategic imperative for the buyer, but instead just an opportunistic idea that fell apart the moment the buyer was distracted by tangential market conditions.

The moral, not to be forgotten: Curve balls come at you in due diligence. Pay attention. Touch all the bases.

CHAPTER 14

AVOIDING SELLER'S REMORSE

What do you want your legacy to be, and how does your business affect that? A business owner's legacy is the sum of many factors: financial goals, of course, but personal, family, community, and charitable factors should also be a consideration. Said this way, to maximize the legacy of your business, there should be more to selling than just maximizing financial return. Thoughtful planning for an exit from your business will maximize your ability to positively affect your legacy. It will also minimize the time required to get the deal done. But one of the most important reasons to make exit planning a priority is to avoid the malady known as seller's remorse.

For many (or most) business owners, their identity is intimately bound to their business. Once the business is no longer there to occupy ten or twelve hours of the day, six or seven days a week, the former business owner finds himself at loose ends. I have seen situations when selling a business leads to what resembles a grief reaction. Letting go of something that has represented a huge investment of time and emotional capital is not easy. Now that the business is ready to live a life of its own, free from the owner/founder, there are bound to be moments of sadness, of regret, of "What if?" It's absolutely normal for the business owner to have these feelings. If it's any consolation, it happens to just about everybody when they exit their business.

What's the way around, or through, these moments of doubt and frustration? Believe it or not, the thought process you used to create a strong business is the same process you use to create a productive life after the sale.

If you've completely left the business and find yourself knocking around the house at loose ends, it's time to break the cycle. Remember when you sat down and wrote a three- to five-year business plan and crafted an exciting, amazing vision for the future of your business? Now that you've hit the ball out of the park, it's time to do the same thing for yourself.

What have you always wanted to do but didn't have time or energy to pursue because you were tied to the business? What are your values? Are you a family person? A spiritual person? Somebody who believes strongly in community service or working for your church? Consider how you can use your skills and talent in service of your values.

Do you have passions, interests, hobbies, or talents you haven't pursued due to lack of time? Consider taking classes at local university extensions or community colleges, or, better yet, volunteer to teach at after-school vocational programs or at the local library. Audition for a role in an amateur theatrical production. Join a choir.

Think outside the office chair.

Seller's remorse may take a different form if you haven't completely exited the business. Perhaps you've agreed to stay on for a while as part of an earn-out, or other structured term of the sale as an employee or consultant. This can make the post-sale transition especially difficult, and it requires a different type of preparation, both psychologically and emotionally.

The point being, it takes strength, maturity, perspective, and self-control to step away from the total commitment you had as an owner and hand the reins to somebody else. Few people are able to make such a transition without wondering whether they did the right thing. If you find yourself in that position, go back to the moment you realized you really and truly wanted to exit the business—not the day you started to think about it, but the precise moment something clicked in your head and started you down the road to sell your company.

It takes strength, maturity, perspective, and self-control to step away from the total commitment you had as an owner.

What were your goals then? Why did you go through the headache, hassle, and expense of preparing your business for the grueling sale process? Write your answers down. Put them in your wallet or in a note on your smartphone. Then refer to that note in moments of shakiness or doubt.

I'm no psychologist, but I know every major life decision can result in moments of doubt: Did I choose the right college? Did I take the right job? Did I buy the right home? Second-guessing decisions is the nature of being human. It doesn't mean you should or should not have chosen the path you chose, it means you're alive, engaged with the world, and open to possibilities.

The time to start planning for your eventual exit is now. More than 50 percent of privately owned businesses will change ownership in the next decade, but three out of four business owners do not have an exit plan. This is a recipe for a cake that won't taste so good.

Having talked with scores (perhaps hundreds) of business owners, I have observed four reasons for the failure to plan for the inevitable exit from their business. First, the business owner does not know where or how to begin. The process seems daunting, and there is no immediate return on investment of the cost and time required to produce a meaningful exit plan. Second, some business owners spend too much time at work putting out fires. Thinking about the future is impossible for them. Third, some business owners assume their business will pass to a family member, and that will somehow just happen when and how it's supposed to happen. Finally, some business owners have difficulty discussing financial matters and personal goals, so they simply avoid the subject of exit planning. My dad was like that. He wasn't the type to sit down and think proactively and prospectively. He would have thought planning for his business exit to be a waste of time.

But the exit planning process has compelling benefits that justify the required time and cost. The process helps a business owner maximize company value because it clarifies strategic options, and it will help the business owner responsibly manage the wealth generated from the sale of the business.

But if the promise of gain does not motivate a business owner, perhaps the threat of pain will do the job. The financial and emotional costs of not planning are extremely high. Without a plan, business owners may not be able to control the timing of their exit. Not planning can also mean a business owner might pay too much in capital gains and income taxes, not to mention estate taxes. The worst effect from the failure to plan is the business owner might leave behind unnecessary headaches for family members. Seriously, what's the upside to failing to plan? The answer would be, there are no upsides for failing to plan.

Some business owners I talk with tell me exit planning sounds good in theory but is too difficult to make happen in practice. They are too busy making the business succeed, so there is no time or money for exit planning. This is miscalculated thinking. It does not add up.

STAN WAS COMMITTED to a carefully crafted exit plan. A very personable fellow who cared deeply about his clients, Stan was a hard worker who owned a profitable financial services consulting company. When we met, Stan was sixty-two years old and had owned the business for eighteen years. He had no strategic plan to exit even though he knew he would need to sell his business sooner than later. Stan was smart enough to realize an exit might choose him before he had a chance to choose how he would exit. So, he committed to the exit-planning process.

His starting point was revenue of $5.5 million and EBITDA of $900,000, which represented a market value of about $5 million. To get that value up would require some work. Stan needed to develop a stronger midlevel management team, improve their sales training program, and modify the reporting and accountability structure. These fundamental changes didn't happen overnight. But, over the course of four years, Stan implemented these improvements and revenue increased to $9 million, cash flow almost doubled, and the company was sold to a foreign strategic buyer for almost $10 million. Four years of planning netted Stan $5 million in added value. And, by the way, not only did this planning process provide more cash at close, it saved Stan $600,000 in capital gains taxes, and he developed an estate plan that saved about $1 million in estate taxes. You might say Stan hit it out of the park.

Business owners can and should control how and when they exit. Careful pre-exit planning will help a business owner maximize value in good times and bad times, reduce their bill to Uncle Sam, shorten the due diligence and documentation periods, and have better control over confidentiality. Choose the legacy you want to leave by planning your exit before you plan to exit.

EPILOGUE

You've always wondered what the views were like at the top of that big building downtown. So here you are, waiting for the lawyers and bankers to arrive to start the closing process. No matter how long you've prepared, this moment will seem like an out-of-body experience. Am I really doing this? Should I be doing this? I can't believe I'm doing this!

Everyone finally arrives, and it's time to start the document signing process. Then comes the moment you've waited for and dreamed about for so long: the wire transfer. If it's timed right, you can often have the wire transfer effective while you wait. You're looking at your bank account online, then boom, there it is, this number hits your account. In a moment, all your doubt goes away and you realize, indeed you *see*, that you have hit your home run. The game is over. You won.

But here's a nuance you probably didn't see coming: your success as a player now turns you into a coach. You see, it won't be long before other business owners and entrepreneur wannabes are asking for your advice. They will want to know your secret, that one thing you did that made the difference.

But you know your home run exit was a combination of many factors. The buyer that found your business irresistible wasn't looking at just one thing. Yogi Berra, the occasional philosopher and baseball great, said it this way: "This ain't football; you can't make up no trick plays." Your home run exit wasn't a trick play, it was the result of years of planning and hard work to intentionally develop an irresistible business. Maybe it was your diverse customer base, perhaps your sustainable revenue stream—your quality financials surely were a consideration, as was your demonstrable scalability. Maybe your buyer was particularly attracted to your unique market position, or your compelling growth story. The fact that the business was not dependent on you also played a huge factor.

Whatever the key factor was, the money's in your account, and the view from the top is breathtaking. The deal's done. If you have a post-exit plan in place, you know what your next step will be. It could be hanging up your cleats and spending time pursuing other passions. Maybe you will coach other business owners to plan their home run exits. Or maybe you will step up to the plate again and start or buy a new business. Only you know for sure. No matter what you choose, you'll always know to lean on the wisdom and intentional focus of the Seven Principles of Irresistibility.

APPENDIX I

BUYING A BUSINESS

I don't think a week goes that I don't get a call that goes something like this: "I want to buy a business. I'm tired of my life in corporate America and I'm ready to be an entrepreneur." Before I talk about opportunities that might be of interest to these callers, I ask a few questions to understand how serious they are about becoming an entrepreneur. Here's why: being an entrepreneur looks glamorous to those who aren't, but I don't know many entrepreneurs who would describe their lives as glamorous. Putting your own money and time at risk in hopes of an eventual economic return is not easy or fun. Contrast that with corporate life: a benefits package, a support system around you, bimonthly automatic deposits into your bank account, and free coffee. I mean, seriously, life in corporate America is pretty darned sweet. Leaving that is the equivalent of Brad Pitt walking away from Jennifer Aniston. It might be the right decision, but think long and hard before you do it. The alternative might not be as great as you think.

Okay, that's a stretch of an analogy, but you get my point. Walking away from a nice gig in corporate America to take on the life of an entrepreneur isn't for everybody.

I have talked with hundreds of would-be business buyers. I wish I had a psychology degree to go along with my law and advanced business degrees. More often than not, the person seeking advice doesn't really want help finding a business to buy. Instead, they need help deciding what to do with the rest of their lives.

Recent disruptions in the American economy have caused more corporate layoffs and uncertainty than in previous eras. Many enterprising businessmen and women have considered escaping the perceived uncertainty of corporate life for the ostensible certainty of "controlling my own destiny." The motivations I hear are generally something like, "I'm too old to find a job that'll replace my income," or "I want to get ahead of the job cuts coming," or the always popular, "I'm ready to be my own boss." Whatever the motivation, the conversation always comes to this: "I'm looking for a good opportunity." So I always respond, "How do you define a good opportunity?" I usually get a blank stare after I ask that question.

A weird phenomenon arises when trying to find a business to buy, which I call the opportunity paradox. Marty was the personification of this. When he called, he got right to the point: "I want to buy a business, I'm looking for a good opportunity." Marty's voice had a sense of urgency. "You have businesses to buy, so you sell businesses, right?"

When people like Marty say they want "a good opportunity," what they're implying is they want a business that will safely replace their income. When pressed for more detail, they usually also say they are looking for a business that is underpriced and owned by someone willing to self-finance. I often hear it described this way, "I'm looking for a retiring business owner who doesn't have a succession plan, and who's willing to bring someone alongside to transition the business over two or three years." Seriously, I've heard that hundreds of times.

So let's say I then have a business for them to look at. Here's what always—and I mean *always*—happens next. Once they have evaluated a business, they come back and tell me all the problems with the business. This is why I call it the opportunity paradox: when you find what you say you want, you don't want it.

That's why I believe people like Marty who say they're "looking for a good opportunity" really just want another job. They are not emotionally suited for the uncertainty of business ownership. They have no appetite for the risks of taking something from point A to point B, much less from point A to point Z.

So I work hard to help aspiring business owners figure out in advance if business ownership is really right for them. After hundreds of conversations like this I've come to believe the one characteristic that best defines an entrepreneur is the ability to be comfortable in a dark room, to have an innate sense that "I can find the light."

Imagine being in a dark room. You don't know where the walls are, if there's a light switch anywhere to be found, if the light switch works, or if there's even a functioning light bulb once you flip the switch.

That's what buying a business is like. There is seldom clarity about how the business will perform. And, the truth is, the life of corporate employment has done little to prepare the aspiring business buyer for a life of uncertainty.

But let's say you really are serious about becoming an entrepreneur. How do you find one of these "opportunities?"

Most people realize that business-for-sale websites are just a slight step up from Craigslist, so where does one really look for a good business to buy? After I graduated from business school, my first boss was the renowned real estate developer Trammell Crow, who used to say, "Luck is being in the right place at the right time, so go get in a lot of places."

The older I get the more I appreciate Mr. Crow's wisdom. Most of the good things that have happened in my life have been the result of just paying attention to what's going on around me. This advice holds true when looking for a business to acquire. Talk to a lot of people. Tell your friends you're looking. Tell bankers, lawyers, and accountants you know. Also, reach out to influencers in your community. When I was at Disney contemplating becoming an entrepreneur, I made an offhand comment to my pastor who connected me with a friend who he knew was interested in selling his radio business in Nashville. Within weeks, I was negotiating to purchase that business.

Another place to look is, surprisingly, bankruptcy court. Many of the businesses in bankruptcy are there not because they're bad businesses, but because they have bad capital structures or dysfunctional management. I once bought a business in a bankruptcy auction that was a good business, but had gotten in trouble because of disagreements between the partners' wives. There are roses amongst the thorns in bankruptcy.

Cast your net far and wide, be open to opportunities that might not at first even look like opportunities.

Okay, let's say you are emotionally ready to make the leap—have you come to grips with the amount of money it is going to take? I have seen many corporate refugees looking to become entrepreneurs who haven't thought through how much capital they are willing to invest in a business, or the kind of risk they are willing to assume.

You see, what drives most corporate refugees looking to buy a business is not how much they want to invest, but how much they want to make in the short term. More often than not, corporate refugees are looking to buy a business that can replace their current salary. But they don't connect the dots between the valuation of a business that delivers the salary they want, and how much that will cost. Here's the logic flaw I see all the time: the prospective buyer will base their EBITDA target on how much they want to make from the business, forgetting that EBITDA drives valuation.

Let's say you want to replace your corporate salary of $300,000 and you find a business with an EBITDA of $1 million. This looks like a great deal! The business makes $1 million, and you want to pay yourself $300,000, which leaves $700,000 for bank payments. But how much will that business cost? Let's say it ranks relatively high on the Seven Principles of Irresistibility, so it will sell for a multiple of six: $6 million. Commercial lenders today might stretch to make a secured loan on a multiple of three, so the bank loan might be as much as $3 million. Assuming that loan has a ten-year term, the annual payment will be around $400,000 (assuming a 6 percent rate of interest). Again, you, the prospective buyer, think this will work. You have $700,000 available for bank payments, and the actual payment will only be $400,000. This deal is looking better and better!

Of course, the buyer may assume the seller will be willing to carry a note so as to reduce the amount of equity required at close, but in today's hyper-competitive environment, the owner of this business is likely to get other offers that do not require a seller's note.

The bottom line is our corporate refugee needs $3 million in cash, plus sufficient borrowing capacity to support the $3 million bank loan. How many people making $300,000 per year have that kind of liquid capital and borrowing capacity? The painful reality: our corporate refugee buyer can't afford the business that will provide the salary, much less the safety, for which he or she is looking.

Here's another conundrum I see all the time, the corporate refugee is so fixated on replacing their corporate income that they miss the perfect opportunity.

When I bought my radio business, I reduced my compensation by 90 percent from the salary I made at Disney. I was buying a business that had problems I knew I could fix, and I was confident those fixes would result in an enormous upside. Admittedly, my wife was a bit concerned (terrified actually, but that's another story). Fortunately, we had savings to ensure our kids didn't go hungry, but we significantly adjusted our lifestyle to make the deal work. Here's the point: my driving consideration when buying the business was *not* about replacing my corporate salary, it was about embracing an opportunity to create long-term value. That's how the successful business buyer has to think.

But buying a business is not the only way to pursue an entrepreneurial dream. You can start a business from an idea, or you can buy a franchise. There is no right or wrong way to approach what's right for you, so let's review each.

STARTING A BUSINESS FROM AN IDEA

Everyone knows the Mark Zuckerberg story by now. Like many young men his age, meeting girls was as much on his mind as his studies. When he was a sophomore at Harvard, he started playing around with an idea that would encourage students to post their picture online (a "face book"). At the time of this writing, fourteen years later, his late-adolescent idea is worth $500 billion, and Zuckerberg's personal fortune is more than $50 billion.

One of the most popular shows on television today is ABC's *Shark Tank*. During its six years on the air, we have seen hundreds of startup ideas, some completely crazy and destined to go nowhere, and some that have become multimillion dollar successes, such as Scrub Daddy and Tipsy Elves.

If you watch a few episodes of *Shark Tank* and write down every question the "sharks" ask, you'll be surprised to see the same themes emerge every time: Is there a problem the idea solves? Does the founder have the skill set and time to get the idea off the ground? Does the idea make a profit? Can the idea grow and, if so, how big can it be?

These questions are the same ones that should be asked of every business start-up. Of course, Mark Zuckerberg couldn't have seen what Facebook would eventually become, but at its core the idea of a "face book" made sense. The market potential was obviously huge—last time I checked, guys still like meeting girls, and girls still like meeting guys.

Indeed, starting a business can be enormously rewarding, but there is a reason failure rates are so high: most startup ideas are fueled by passion instead of common-sense answers to questions like you hear on *Shark Tank*. Almost every major city in America has some kind of organized resource to help entrepreneurs launch new businesses. In my area, it's the Nashville Entrepreneurial Center. Organizations like this help entrepreneurs think through the hard questions and even help them meet potential investment sources. But it's a lonely road from idea in the shower to ringing NASDAQ's opening bell.

Maybe worse than being lonely, that road is also unpredictable. I recently helped two guys sell a business they started just five years earlier. They had an idea that resonated immediately, and within five years they were making $2 million in annual profit. We sold the company to a private equity firm for an eight-figure valuation. Nice story, right? Conversely, I was also recently engaged to sell a software product that my client spent $3 million to create. It was a good product, and he had forty customers paying a $9,000 per year license fee. Unfortunately, the product didn't have the profit margin to fund the marketing efforts needed to find a wide base of customers. We might have been able to sell the software, but likely not for anywhere near the $3 million my client invested (not to mention the past six to seven years of his life dedicated to the business).

Both of these startup ideas were logical, and the founders had passion and know-how. One made it big fast, the other continues to flounder. Can you figure out in advance why/how this will happen? Perhaps, but only if you get answers to the hard questions about market demand, profit margins, and total cost required to go from idea to market. When I am asked to evaluate a *pro forma* for a start-up, I tell the founder to double his expense expectations and cut his revenue projection in half. If the model still makes sense at that point, then go forward.

Let me say it this way: just because you have a good idea doesn't mean you're guaranteed to have a good business. You can't cross the ocean in a rowboat (well, maybe you can, but it's dangerous), so before you go out on your startup journey, make sure you are equipped with solid answers to the hard questions.

BUYING A FRANCHISE

Buying a franchise has elements of both investing in a start-up and buying an existing business. Buying a franchise allows you to go into business *for* yourself but not *by* yourself. The theory behind buying a franchise is that you are buying a business model that has worked elsewhere. But the franchise approach also has elements of a startup because you will be the one doing the work to set the business up and get it rolling.

Keep in mind, when you buy a franchise, you are not buying a business; you are buying the right to replicate a business in a given location. There are hundreds of franchise opportunities for selling products and services that range from bug control to organic hamburgers. You can attend franchise conferences, find a franchise broker, or just ask owners of other franchises how they found theirs. There are tons of resources available to help you think through the pros and cons of buying a franchise, so I won't belabor them here. But I will warn you about two things based on my own experience having once bought a franchise. First, remember that buying a franchise is like buying a job that requires direct selling. If you have never wanted to be in sales, you probably don't want to own a franchise. The franchisor will tell you to "follow the system," implying there's a foolproof method to be successful. But you still have to find the location, hire the staff, and find the customers. And that last one—finding the customers—means one thing: you are in sales. With the possible exception of some food franchises (Subway, Panera, etc.), once you have opened your franchise, *you* have to go out and bring the customers in. I enjoy doing that, though not everyone does, and it's often the reason franchises fail.

Second, do not assume the system you are buying will work in your market. What makes the system work in Florida, Maine, or Colorado may not apply in your market. Moreover, the franchisor will probably not help you evaluate the competitive opportunity in your locale. There might already be strong competitors in the market area you are considering. So remember, just because the franchise is *available* in your area does not mean it will work in your area; what works in one area may not always work in another.

Another problem I see is prospective franchise buyers tend to evaluate opportunities based on what they like versus what's a good competitive fit for their market. Following passion is good when picking a spouse, but it should be secondary when picking a business opportunity.

Finally, too many prospective franchise buyers fail to ask the hard questions of themselves: Am I willing to do the required work day in and day out? How long will it take for the franchise to deliver the compensation I need? How much do I really need to invest to get there?

Taking the leap from corporate life to being an entrepreneur is harder than most people think, and there is no test to determine one's readiness. Based on my experience, and seeing scores of others do it, I know for certain that unless you are willing to sacrifice blood and sweat, and live with fear, you should not become an entrepreneur. Though there will always be the spectacular successes like Mark Zuckerberg, the road to entrepreneurial success is long, curvy, and full of uncertainty.

Entrepreneurs have to be precise in their thinking, challenge every assumption, and plan conservatively. But, at the same time, the road to entrepreneurial success is paved with inspiration and an unfailing belief in one's ability to succeed. Therein lies the paradox of becoming an entrepreneur: the need to be a critical thinker exists simultaneously with the need to be willing to jump out of the plane.

SEVEN PRINCIPLES OF IRRESISTIBILITY TEST

ANSWER EACH QUESTION WITH A NUMBER FROM 0 TO 5.

0	1	2	3	4	5

No   Not Sure   Yes, I think   Absolutely Certain

Diverse customer base

_____ Is your largest customer less than 20 percent of your revenue?

_____ Does 60 percent or more of your revenue come from more than one industry?

Sustainable revenue stream

_____ Can you predict the next twelve months' revenue with reasonable accuracy?

_____ Do your customers buy your core product/ service on a regular basis?

Reliable financial statements

_____ Does a third-party accountant audit your annual financials?

_____ Are your financials GAAP-compliant?

Demonstrable scalability

_____ Is your profit growing faster than your revenue?

_____ As you grow revenue, does your cost of goods sold go down as a percentage of revenue?

_____ Does your overhead as a percentage of revenue go down when you grow revenue?

Unique market position

_____ When you tell people what you do, do they seem impressed?

_____ Do you have a distinctive, easy-to-articulate edge over your top competitor?

_____ Can you charge more than your competitors because of something special about your service/product?

Owner independence

_____ In the past two years, have you taken a vacation of two weeks or longer?

_____ If you were unable to work for the next six months, would revenue go down more than 10 percent?

_____ Do you have a system of doing business that your employees understand and follow?

Believable growth story

_____ Do you have a formula to know if you invest a certain amount in marketing it will return a definable amount of revenue?

_____ Can you articulate how to reach your target customer?

_____ Do you maintain regular metrics to understand your business?

SCORE	HOW BUYER PERCEIVES YOU	IMPACT ON YOUR MULTIPLE
<20	Damaged	Reduce by 50 percent or more
21-45	Problem	Reduce by 20-35 percent
46-60	Solid	Likely no impact
61-80	Attractive	Add 20-35 percent
81+	Irresistible	Add 50 percent or more

ACKNOWLEDGMENTS

I have thought about writing a book for years, and I am glad I finally took the time to do it. But boy howdy, it isn't an easy process. Writing a book requires hundreds of hours thinking, organizing, writing, editing, and then more editing. A lot of time not spent with family or on the golf course. It's ironic that writing a book is such a lonely process, because the result is something that hopefully can help many people.

The good folks of Advantage Media Group were invaluable in their encouragement and direction. Helping first-time authors like me entitles them to a special place in heaven. I could not have done this without your prodding and advice, offered every time with kindness and enthusiasm. To you I cannot say thanks enough.

I am blessed over the years to have many mentors who have helped me grow personally and professionally. Kit Bond, John Ashcroft, Joe Frappier, Woody Coley, Todd Mansfield, Maurice Templeton, and Joe Davis are men with whom I have been honored to work. They pushed me to be better at whatever I was doing, and I am grateful for their influence in my business life.

My wife Emily Elizabeth (Underwood) Cumbee is the inspiration that drives me every day. Hey, Dear, please don't tell anyone how cranky I was those months I was writing this book. Let's keep that a secret just between us. I love you very much.

Every dad wants his kids to be proud of him. Sam, Mary, and Matthew, I am so grateful for each of you, and I hope this book makes you proud.

This book would not have been possible without the interactions I've had with hundreds of business owners. From each of you I have learned something—sometimes good, sometimes not so good. I hope my input into your business life has been productive.

Finally, I am grateful to serve a loving God who sent His son Jesus to redeem a lost world. Through faith in Jesus Christ as my personal savior, I am able to take on life's challenges with gusto and hope. To John Wright, Jim Henry, Jimmy Knott, and Mike Glenn, your spiritual influence and encouragement has helped me see that whatever talents God has given me should ultimately be used for His glory. That seems about right, because it is to Him that I owe it all.

ABOUT THE AUTHOR

Jim Cumbee is one of the most trusted business brokers throughout the Tennessee Valley. He has more than thirty years experience as a successful entrepreneur and senior corporate executive. Jim has an MBA from Harvard Business School, a JD from the University of Missouri at Kansas City School of Law, and a BA in history from Westminster College. He has held senior level executive positions with Disney Development Company (a division of the Walt Disney Company), Salem Communications, and Reach Satellite Network. He and his wife Emily have been married for thirty-three years, and have three adult children and two grandchildren (he'll be happy to show you pictures).

To inquire about speaking engagements or bulk orders of this book, contact Jim at (615) 390-9966 or jim@tnvalleygroup.com.